D1088764

Louis Kahn

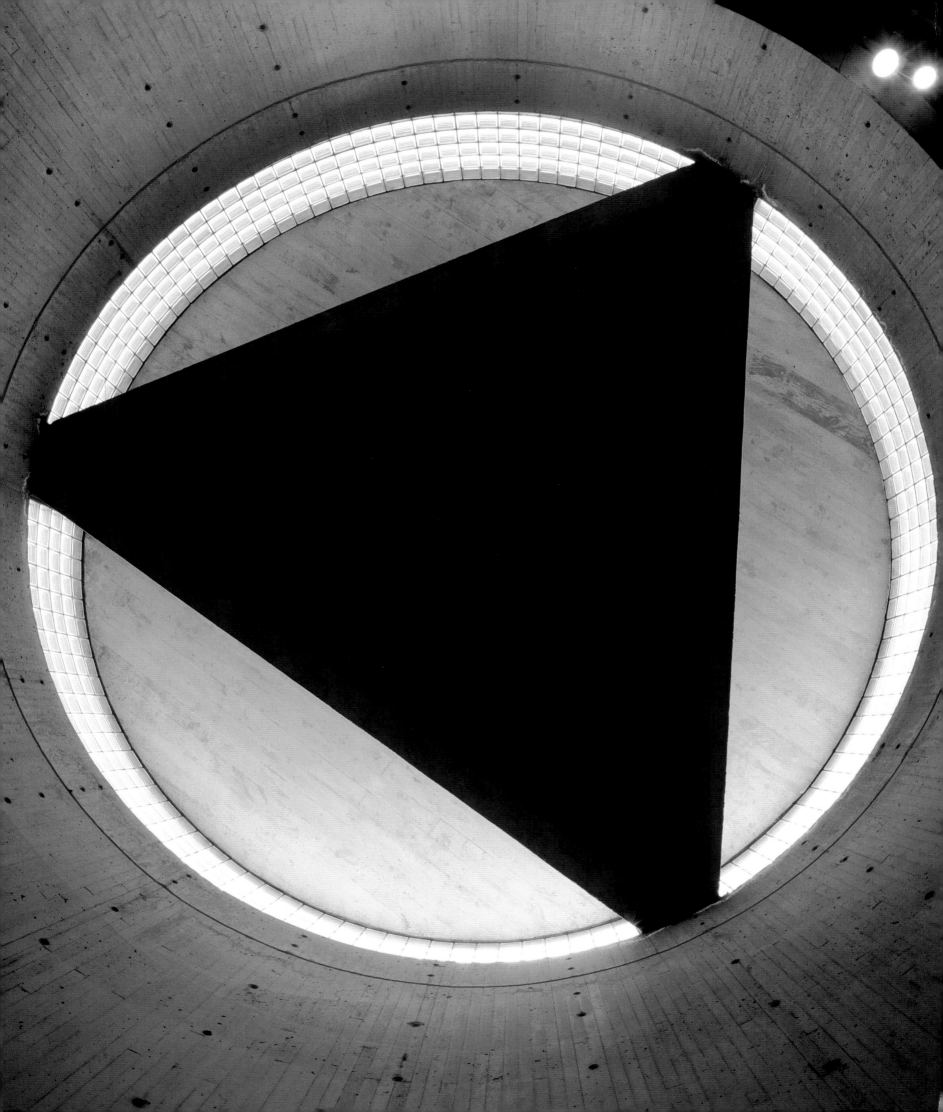

Louis Kahn

Joseph Rykwert

New photography by Roberto Schezen

Harry N. Abrams, Inc., Publishers

NA
737
.K32
R94
2001

Editor: Diana Murphy
Designer: Judy Hudson

Library of Congress Cataloging-in-Publication Data
Rykwert, Joseph, 1926–
Louis Kahn / Joseph Rykwert ; photographs by Roberto Schezen.
    p. cm.
ISBN 0–8109–4226–7
1. Kahn, Louis I., 1901–1974—Criticism and interpretation. 2. Architecture—United States—20th century. I. Kahn, Louis I., 1901–1974. II. Title.
NA737.K32 R94 2001
720'.92—dc21   2001001354

Text © 2001 Joseph Rykwert
Except as otherwise noted in photograph credits, photographs © 2001 Roberto Schezen

Published in 2001 by Harry N. Abrams, Incorporated, New York
All rights reserved. No part of the contents of this book may be reproduced without the written permission of the publisher.

Printed and bound in Japan

Harry N. Abrams, Inc.
100 Fifth Avenue
New York, N.Y. 10011
www.abramsbooks.com

Page 1:
Yale University Art Gallery, detail of the wall surface in the stair cylinder
Page 2:
Yale University Art Gallery, view of the ceiling from the main stairway
Pages 6–7:
Salk Institute, view to the west
Pages 8–9:
Phillips Exeter Academy Library, central hall

LONGWOOD COLLEGE LIBRARY
REDFORD AND PINE ST.
FARMVILLE, VA 23909

Contents

Louis Kahn: An Introduction

The publication of this book coincides with the centenary of Louis Kahn's birth, though its immediate occasion is the new collection of images that illustrate this text and provide an opportunity to reconsider his achievement and his way of working. Although Kahn was born in 1901, his fame and his best work really belong to the next generation. All the buildings that made him famous and gained him international recognition as one of the great innovative figures of world architecture were done after he passed fifty, and they are associated with two radical notions to which he attached great importance: the first is that any sound building must be rooted in its materiality and be proudly true to the way it is made; the second is a conviction that however important the house, the factory, or the office may be – both as types and as elements in the configuration of the city – architecture must nonetheless concern itself primarily with the anatomy of society, and therefore with its institutions. His most important buildings were churches, synagogues, universities, and museums.

Kahn's father had come to the United States by himself, to be soon followed by his wife and the five-year-old Louis in 1906. Although Kahn could have no very clear memories of his childhood home on the Estonian island of Saaremaa (which defines and shelters the Gulf of Riga – part of the Russian Empire at the time), he was fascinated by this shadowy background. This "Finnish Jew," as he called himself, was as quintessentially American as an exact contemporary of his, also a child of poor Russian-Jewish refugees who had an equally bracing effect on American art – Aaron Copland.

Their careers were quite different, however. Copland was born in Brooklyn, but when he was barely out of his teens, he was sent to Paris to study with Nadia Boulanger, whose classes were the rite of passage and qualifying passport to the musical avant-garde in Europe as in America. In contrast, Kahn, though his precocious drawing talent was quickly recognized, was trained in his hometown, Philadelphia, under Paul Philippe Cret, who – as a very successful new graduate of the Ecole des Beaux-Arts in Paris – had been headhunted by the University of Pennsylvania to reorganize its school of architecture along authentic Parisian lines. Although Cret concentrated much more on a rigorous analytical and planning method than on the business of ornament and stylistic fidelity, his teaching followed the main lines of the doctrines imparted at the Ecole – the analysis of the program into an axial composition, the use of gridded structures, and so on. Nor did he ever depart from them – his mastery of that method was, after all, his main attraction for his Philadelphian employers. Kahn, too, was trained in that discipline, and he remained personally loyal to his teacher though not to his teacher's method.[1] He also remained attached to, even passionately involved with, Philadelphia, with its clear and sagacious grid plan, which had been set out by William Penn, its founder, in the seventeenth century. This involvement was a leitmotif that returned throughout his life.

Cret may have been more open to recent developments in architecture than many of his contemporaries, yet his own work only edged far enough out of the conventional academic pieties to flirt with a sober, accomplished version of Art Deco. As a student Kahn produced very good, but not outstanding, work. That could also be said about many of his early projects: very good, but not outstanding. Upon graduating from college, he went

Yale Center for British Art,
entrance court, wall detail

directly into the city architect's office, and what with that and some other jobs, he had soon saved enough money to undertake the European study trip that was – then as now – part of every ambitious architect's training. The Mediterranean was his principal destination – as it was for most such travelers – yet he began his journey on his own native island. The cool, bare, solemn architecture of Estonian castles and churches impressed Kahn almost as much as the warm grandeur of the Mediterranean, the expected masterpieces of Italy, and the treasures of popular building he discovered for himself.

His return route took him through Paris, and the city's vitality offered him an ideal of urban life – another important lesson. Perhaps he was more like George Gershwin (whose music he loved to play) than like the cosmopolitan Copland (whom he certainly knew). On his return to the United States in the spring of 1929, he briefly found work in Cret's office. He also married the handsome, intelligent, and much-courted student of psychology, Esther Israeli. All this did something to counteract his shyness, which was partly due to the fact that a childhood fire-accident had left the lower half of his face heavily scarred. Any ambitious plans the young couple might have had were to be curtailed, however. It was the Depression, and soon Cret's office had to shrink. Work for all architects in the next few years was sporadic, and Kahn was compelled to live with his parents-in-law.

Also in 1929 one of the century's most remarkable American buildings, the Philadelphia Savings Fund Society's headquarters, was begun in that city. The thirty-story skyscraper known acronymically as the PSFS was designed by George Howe and William Lescaze. The patrician Howe had been educated at the Ecole des Beaux-Arts in Paris and was already known for some handsome stone "traditional" buildings, although he was now moving toward a sparer and recognizably modern manner shorn of historical echoes. He had gone into partnership with the Swiss-trained "modernist"

Lescaze (who had been working in the United States for a decade) to conceive a building that had nothing in common with the jazzy Art Deco skyscrapers going up in New York just before the Depression. A sober, carefully molded volume, the PSFS maintained the street line at ground level, where a shop-ringed hall was linked to a subway entrance. Above it an airy, three-story-high banking chamber was the podium of a vertically articulated rectilineal block. At the summit there was a large electric sign and a directors' penthouse. The PSFS has been called the first modern skyscraper; it was also one of the earliest to be air-conditioned.

Yet the Lescaze-Howe partnership did not last. While the PSFS building was going up in the aftermath of the Depression and work was scarce, Lescaze left for New York. A few of the younger members of that office (as well as that of Cret) and some of the younger unemployed architects formed a kind of discussion group, of which the very gregarious Kahn was one of the animators; another was his lifelong friend Norman Rice, with whom he had stayed in Paris during his grand tour at a time when Rice was working for Le Corbusier. Howe had also started a short-lived architectural periodical, the *T-Square Club Journal*, which published articles by both Kahn and Rice and was later taken over by R. Buckminster Fuller, who changed its name to *Shelter* before closing it down.

Meanwhile, The Museum of Modern Art in New York had staged its influential show *Modern Architecture: International Exhibition* in 1932 (it later traveled to Philadelphia), which proposed a version of modern architecture as a new style, a formal expedient – quite sanitized of any social or political concerns. As the first such survey in the United States it must have seemed very exciting, and its implications were not evident then. Whatever he thought of it, Kahn at this time was primarily concerned with low-income housing, which had indeed become the dominant theme for most architects during the late 1920s and 1930s – and there were a number of housing projects in the MoMA exhibition and its catalogue. The interest in housing directed his attention to Le Corbusier's and Walter Gropius's work. As it happened, Oscar Stonorov – who may have been a few years Kahn's junior, but had studied in Florence and was (like Lescaze) a graduate of the Zürich Polytechnic, had won a prize in the Palace of the Soviets competition, coedited the first volume of Le Corbusier's *Oeuvre* (with his Swiss partner, Willi Boesiger), and had the worldly polish Kahn lacked – moved to Philadelphia in 1929. With his German partner, Alfred Kastner, he was commissioned by the Hosiery Workers' Union to design the first "modern" housing project in the city, and it was built in 1932–35. Kahn's own low-cost housing projects, garden-city–type *Siedlungen*, had been designed in the hope – which was disappointed – of funding from the Works Progress Administration. They were still closer in manner to the English rather than to the Continental work of the time.

In 1934–35 Kahn was beginning to receive individual commissions, including one for a small synagogue – his first institutional building. Kastner, who had meanwhile moved to Washington, D.C., involved him in another *Siedlung*-type development, for the resettlement of New York garment workers between Princeton and Trenton, New Jersey, as a commune. Much of it was built, and this time the WPA helped. Kahn spent eighteen months on the project but returned to Philadelphia in mid-1937. His work was limited (even if the synagogue was already under construction), but it was the time when large-scale public housing was a New Deal priority. Howe set up an office to handle such work, and called in Kahn as a planner-designer. His most ambitious project (for some 1,500 housing units) was, unfortunately, defeated by the combined opposition of local residents and the city government to such New Deal policies.

With the approach of war, there was increasing pressure, even before Pearl Harbor, to provide emergency housing for war workers. Howe set up a partnership with Kahn, and they developed a number of low-rise, quite high-density settlement projects, which Kahn, for his part, would not treat as an emergency makeshift but assumed would become the prototypes for housing to be built after the war. Both Howe and Kahn experimented with a number of alternative plans and built some large housing complexes, two of which, at Pennypack Woods, near Philadelphia, and Carver Court, in Caln Township in that city's suburbs, were widely published and helped gain Kahn national recognition as an expert on low-income housing. Howe and Kahn then took Stonorov into the partnership, and when Howe became head of the Federal Housing Administration in Washington, D.C., Stonorov – who had long worked with labor unions – and Kahn continued collaborating even after the urgency of war work had receded.

Had Kahn either changed careers or died before 1950, his name would have been worth little more than a footnote in the story of twentieth-century American architecture. As it was, his work was moving almost imperceptibly – and a little gawkily – away from the prevailing "modern" commonplaces of the time, perfectly exemplifying the observation that "originality consists in trying to do just like everybody else without quite succeeding."[2] That is why it is easy to present him as a historicist, as a worthy product of Beaux-Arts teaching – as if he had not been its glorious failure. Or, as he put it himself more gently, "I have spent all my time since graduation unlearning what I have learned."[3]

In the mid-1940s, large-scale reconstruction, the replacing of housing stock destroyed during World War II, seemed the obvious priority for architects throughout the world. Yet there was also a growing interest in the possibility of a new kind of monumental architecture, one that was not historically conditioned but grew out of the best of the avant-garde work of the 1930s. It was fostered at the end of the war by Sigfried Giedion and Lewis Mumford – with the help of Josep Lluis Sert and Fernand Léger – and marked the end of the purely utilitarian, "functionalist" view of modernity. Increasingly after this time, and from different directions, there came demands for an architecture that would not merely satisfy physical and economic needs, but also would attempt to cater to psychological, even spiritual ones. Kahn had tried to clarify this very issue some years earlier in his first theoretical piece of writing: monumentality, he said, "is a spiritual quality inherent in a structure which conveys a feeling of its eternity – it cannot be added to or changed."[4] Although Kahn did not get closer to a definition, his polemic in this essay (which appeared as part of a symposium on architecture and city planning published in 1944) was directed against those who related monumentality to "traditional" materials; he argued for the use of steel, of plastics, of new forms of glass, and singled out welded and tubular structures (so much more elegant than bolted or riveted ones) in institutional building. Monumentality, Kahn wrote, "cannot be intentionally created" in any case.

Working conditions for architects were to change after the war as the boom in emergency housing was phased out. Kahn established his Philadelphia office, and his commissions were almost all for private houses. They tended to have free plans and were built with heavy, random masonry load-bearing walls – not unlike the houses Marcel Breuer was building at the time. In 1944 Kahn had also been invited to extend a sizeable public building, the Philadelphia Psychiatric Hospital, on which he worked intermittently until 1954. A building boom was expected, and building manufacturers and magazines launched a flurry of "ideas" competitions. Kahn used them to develop some of his more unorthodox concepts. Paradoxically, it was his work on housing that led to a rising interest in institutions as the prime concern of architecture. From this followed his conviction that monumentality can only be an attribute of buildings of a public nature.

In 1945 Kahn and Stonorov were asked by the Philadelphia City Planning Commission to draw up plans for an underdeveloped area of the city known as the "Triangle." Its side was constituted by the railway lines

(they would run up to the town hall until 1929, though the viaduct that carried them and was known as the "Chinese Wall" and long due for demolition was still standing in 1945); its base was the Schuylkill River; and its hypotenuse the Benjamin Franklin Parkway, diagonal to the city grid. Kahn was largely responsible for the graphic presentation of the group's proposals. They do not show any spectacular innovations as yet, but in proper International Style fashion they involve some zoning and the building of a number of sizeable slab-blocks in parkland. The exhibition in 1947 at which these plans were publicly displayed was a great success, though unfortunate disputes about credit led to a break with Stonorov.

By this time Kahn was also recognized as a demanding and inspiring teacher. He had already taught ad hoc (as at Harvard, for instance), and in 1945 accepted an appointment at Yale. He also persuaded his old associate and friend Howe to head the architecture school there – which he did with great success, though when the offer to succeed Howe was made to Kahn in 1956, he would not accept the appointment. By then Kahn had already been made a professor at his alma mater, the University of Pennsylvania, and his studio was becoming a place of international pilgrimage. Students were attracted by the increasing respect for his work, but also by the fame of his ruthless and steady questioning of the building process, and his dogged search for worthy and relevant ways of representing the institutions of society. His reluctance to make any unfavorable comments on student work was celebrated. His opinion of a project could be estimated, it is said, by the length of the silence in the studio while he tried to think of a just and appropriate positive remark.

Like all major artists, Kahn was also a sharp and perceptive critic of his contemporaries: what he had to say on Frank Lloyd Wright, on Ludwig Mies van der Rohe, and on Alvar Aalto is always worth reading. He was also in sympathy with those who were apparently pursuing quite different ends, like Carlo Scarpa, for instance. But he always looked over his shoulder at the one figure who seemed to him to tower over his own time, and would constantly ask himself, "How am I doin', Corbusier?"[5]

Though generously committed to teaching, Kahn now ran his own practice, and had enough work for a small but busy office. A young and strong-minded Harvard graduate, Anne Tyng, joined it in 1945, and brought with her a passionate interest in geometry as a generator of architectural form. She would become, as Fuller put it, his "geometrical strategist."[6] Kahn's incipient interest in such working methods was also fostered through his growing friendship with the great French engineer Robert Le Ricolais, a pioneer of three-dimensional structure, who had also accepted a teaching post at the University of Pennsylvania and whose associate, August Komendant, would become Kahn's regular structural engineer.

A gentle hiatus in Kahn's development was provided in 1950 by a three-month stint at the American Academy in Rome, followed by a trip to Greece and Egypt. But by then he did not want long absences from his office or from Philadelphia. The Philadelphia Housing Authority had invited him to work on a large-scale planning and public housing project at Mill Creek, on the western side of the city, which was reduced in scale and ambition over the years. Built in two stages on a very tight budget over the next decade, it included three high-rises, rows of two- and three-story houses, and a community center. At the same time Yale University, where he had been teaching, commissioned him (on Howe's urging, while Kahn was away in Rome) to design a relatively modest but prominently sited building – an extension for the University Art Gallery, of which I will have more to say. This was his first move to a new kind of architecture. Unlike much of his earlier work, the Yale University Art Gallery is very tightly and simply organized. Kahn's future buildings would come to be distinguished from his earlier work, as well as that of many contemporaries, by the crisp, insistent geometry of their volumes and the manifest clarity of the struc-

tural detail. It is perhaps no accident that the change of direction came directly after his return from his renewed experience of the great Mediterranean monuments.

Soon after finishing the Yale gallery in 1953, Kahn was commissioned to design the Adath Jeshurun Synagogue at Elkins Park in north Philadelphia, a triangular building in a circular plaza in which he developed the tetrahedral forms that had first appeared in the Yale project. Work was never started on it; however, he did build a more conventionally structured Medical Services Center for the American Federation of Labor and Congress of Industrial Organizations (AFL–CIO) in Philadelphia, which was knocked down to make way for a highway expansion in 1973.

In 1954 he was asked to design the Jewish Community Center in Ewing Township, near Trenton, New Jersey. The commission was probably prompted by a Yale-trained Trenton lawyer who knew of Kahn's work through university publications. Like many other such centers, it was a secular affair with many sports and social facilities but no synagogue or cultual space. The early schemes for this project were developed as a network of polygons, each one covered by a pyramidal pavilion roof. In the end, apart from an open-air camp facility, only the bathhouse, originally intended as changing rooms and showers for the swimming pool, was actually built. It was made up of a Swiss-cross plan of five square (30-by-30-foot) pavilions, four of them covered by a truncated (to allow for an oculus) pyramidal roof each, with the fifth as an open square court between them. Each major square is served at its corners by another four 8-by-8-foot squares, which allow for different entrances (to separate the men's from the women's locker rooms, and so on) and accommodate washrooms and storage. They wrap around the steel columns that support the structure. The concrete-block walls stop short of the underside of the roofs, allowing the main spaces to be lit naturally, as do those of the smaller "servant" spaces, so that the roof structure seems to be lightly hovering above them. It is a small, bare, poor building, yet in it Kahn worked out most of the relation between served and servant spaces, which was later to occupy him most explicitly.

Philadelphia had grown in the immediate postwar period, and it went on growing even more rapidly through the 1950s. Further work on a plan to regulate the expansion and bring some order to the center seemed urgent. The Triangle project had been published in 1948. Although it quickly became obvious that the piecemeal development of the area known as Center City would not follow this or any other plan, Kahn was involved with some of the other consultants on providing variants to guide developers and the city authorities. Meanwhile, the Committee for Municipal Improvement of the Philadelphia Chapter of the American Institute of Architects invited Kahn to reconsider the traffic pattern of the city. This became the extended project whose publication gave him more international

fame than any of his executed buildings, since he was almost alone at the time in thinking through urban problems by relating traffic patterns to public buildings without the usual concentration on housing. In it, Kahn considered traffic flow not just in the light of efficiency but in formal terms as well. Using a sign language that he devised, he contrasted the chaotic and unregulated movement of the automobile, which was destroying the majestic order of Penn's grid plan of the city and disrupting its public space, with that of other vehicles and people on foot. The system employed graded patterns to indicate speed and motion: a meander for pedestrians; staccato, stop-go for shopping and mass transit; and a continuous flow for the automobile. This was supplemented by the creation of a barrier against traffic excess in the form of cylindrical silo buildings for automobiles at the city edge, ramped into what he called "spiral streets"; they were emulated in several later urban projects.

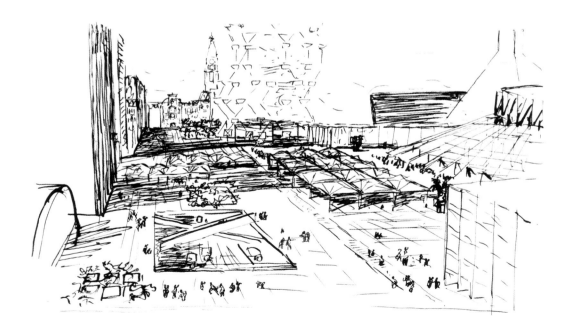

Civic Center, Philadelphia, dominated by the projected City Tower and, behind it, the old City Hall with its statue of William Penn on the spire. ca. 1957

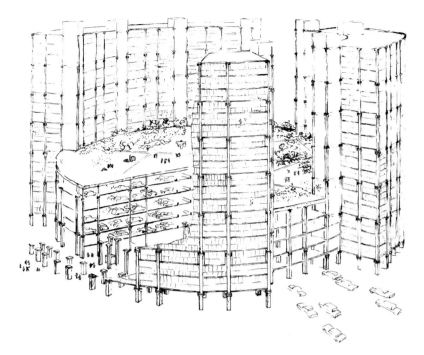

Civic Center, Philadelphia. The parking silos: circular stacked parking platforms were to be surrounded by hotels and department stores. ca. 1957

Kahn worked for much of the next decade on the Center City plan. It was articulated by great public buildings, designed to take up new structural forms and exploit technical innovations, especially the use of three-dimensional, diagonally braced grids. He was looking very carefully at patterns of plant and animal growth as well as the geometries of structure at that time. The most remarkable of these schemes are several variants on the new multifaceted City Hall building, which came to be called City Tower, a light structure that allowed for lofty public spaces, open through several floors, within the cage of the diagonal frame.

Although the concern with the possibilities of three-dimensional structures remained a poetic inspiration, Kahn never built anything as radical as had been proposed by that Philadelphia project and was content to exploit the potentialities of orthogonality in his later work. The more ambitious plans of the early 1950s had even less chance of being realized than the conventional plan of the Philadelphia Triangle, and after 1953 Kahn gradually withdrew to a consultative role in town-planning matters. Yet he continued working on projects for his city, and in 1956 began to elaborate a more

visionary scheme, in which the whole city was enclosed in a series of inhabited viaducts that would also accommodate various forms of transportation as well as parking structures – but above all would act as carriers of water and other main services above ground. He certainly considered his proposals an emulation of the scale of Roman aqueducts and their relation to urban texture. A geometric device was to reappear on the later plans: an equilateral triangle inscribed in a circle. Here it is sketched as a circular hotel tower, with a triangular department store within. In the Yale gallery it encloses the main staircase – and the same geometric device governs the near-contemporary project for the Adath Jeshurun Synagogue in Philadelphia, in which the main triangular building stands within a circular earthwork. In all of these projects, the angles where the triangle touches the circumference of the circle become entry points in the plan.

Kahn was gradually becoming recognized as a national figure. In 1956–57 he participated in a limited competition for a new university library for Washington University in St. Louis, Missouri. His project for a strangely cruciform stepped-pyramid was not the winning one, but it showed him devising yet another application of a regular geometric pattern to a complex program. There were also executed commissions. In 1958 Kahn designed a small and out-of-the-way building for the Tribune Review Publishing Company in Greensburg, Pennsylvania. It was completed in 1961. A low building, it shows Kahn working out some of the implications of his first projects: the *parti* is an enlarged version of the Yale University Art Gallery – two long (1-by-3) machine halls are separated by the service area, which runs as a passage from the main entrance, itself overshadowed by the bulk of the cooling tower. The concern to avoid glare at the work level led him to evolve the window type that would reappear often as a large, hooded area of glass – rectangular at Greensburg, but sometimes semicircular (as in the Performing Arts Theater in Fort Wayne, Indiana, or in the Indian and Bangladeshi buildings) – positioned high in the wall, with a narrow strip window below it, usually at the center and descending to floor level, making a kind of T-shape. Characteristic, too, is the emphatic vertical articulation of the long and low Tribune Review building, which in a sense "asked" to be horizontally treated.

In 1961 Kahn was again called to act as a consultant on another project for developing a part of Philadelphia, but by then he had lost confidence in both the city planners and the authorities to whom they answered. Yet he always remained very clear about the nature of the urban experience. The walled city (he often mentioned Carcassonne) was a model to which he constantly appealed – cities without gateways and expressways to channel traffic out of their centers were as ridiculous as "cities without entrances," he would reiterate.[7] Within the urban enclosure the public building would become the positive marker of city grandeur and prosperity. All this was a declaration about the essential nature of public and urban space.

Comparing Kahn's aerial perspectives of Philadelphia to Giovanni Battista Piranesi's views of Rome (particularly those of the Campo Marzio), as is often done, seems to me to miss the point. Kahn was not preaching nostalgia for past grandeurs, but projecting an immediately realizable future city protected from the excesses of automobile traffic, yet linked to a modern transport system. However, he certainly saw – and

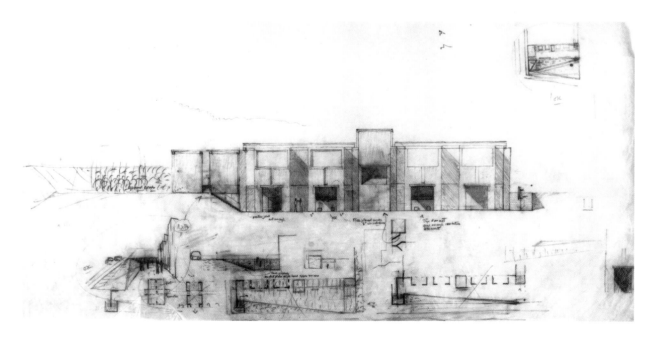

Tribune Review Building, Greensburg, Pennsylvania. Elevation and plan sketches. 1958–61

admired – some of Claude-Nicolas Ledoux's projects: "Ledoux has this feeling of what a town is like, of what a city is like, but he projected this [slide] and 'town' didn't look that way at all. . . . He imagined this."[8] It was Ledoux's forward-looking energy, not Piranesi's nostalgia, that inspired Kahn.

He did appeal to the past, of course, and his taste for the work of certain architects – Ledoux and Etienne-Louis Boullée, Filippo Brunelleschi and Andrea Palladio – shows a Kahn who (unlike many architects of the previous two generations) was very conscious of his position in history. On the one hand, there was no nostalgia in his talk about ancient Rome – or Carcassonne, for that matter. There was never a question of a need to appeal to direct sources, no question ever of any eclectic mixing in his designing. On the other hand, he was always searching for invariant, perpetual principles. He would sometimes equate that search with one for origins, and even confessed to buying multivolume works on history in which he would only read the first few chapters, usually those of volume one. What he really wanted to read though was the as-yet-unwritten volume zero of such a book, in which he might learn the sense of wonder characteristic of beginnings.

In the last decade of his life Kahn received several important commissions. These included, in 1962, the Mikveh Israel Synagogue in central Philadelphia (just off Independence Mall), which went through many versions and in which Kahn first experimented with the circular light-walls he would call "light-bottles"; and in 1965 the motherhouse for the Dominican nuns' congregation of St. Catherine de Ricci in Delaware County, Pennsylvania, on which he worked until 1968, producing a project in which the overlapping of rectangles was elaborated into an extraordinary scatter of public spaces held in by the three-sided rectangle of the cloister and the cells. A year later he was commissioned to do another monastery, St. Andrew's, in Valyermo, California. None of these was even begun.

Nor were two very different commissions – for highrise buildings. One was on a prominent site in New York City, on Broadway between Fifty-sixth and Fifty-seventh Streets, on land owned by the United Church of Christ (formerly known as the Broadway Tabernacle) and now famous as the location of the Hard Rock Café. The first building Kahn proposed was to have battered walls and a complex, almost informal plan; but the church remained on its site, and the highrise would have had a large niche to accommodate it. A few months later Kahn was asked to design an office tower in Kansas City, Missouri, for a developer, Altgar Enterprises. With Komendant again, he devised a form of slip construction that allowed him to raise the main structural members to the top of the building, supporting them on the central core and slender corner elements, and suspending the floors within that skeleton. By using a similar structural form on Broadway, the accommodation of the church on the site would have become much easier. But the developers were frightened by the unorthodox construction, and the project was abandoned and the church destroyed. Fifteen years later a similar, if structurally much less innovative, solution was adopted for the more intransigent St. Peter's Lutheran Church by Hugh Stubbins when he built the Citicorp building on the church's grounds – a commission for which Kahn had been considered. Nonetheless, Kahn continued to elaborate his plans for the Kansas City building and to study the structural problems in great detail, though in 1974 the clients simply withdrew and handed the commission to the huge commercial office of Skidmore, Owings and Merrill. Kahn was left bitter and very disappointed by this outcome.

These developers' buildings did not absorb him as much as two memorials, both for New York City: one, remembering the victims of the Holocaust (called "To the Six Million Jewish Martyrs"), to be composed of nine glass pylons and set in Battery Park, occupied him between 1966 and 1972 – and in spite of the promoters' enthusiasm was never financed; the other,

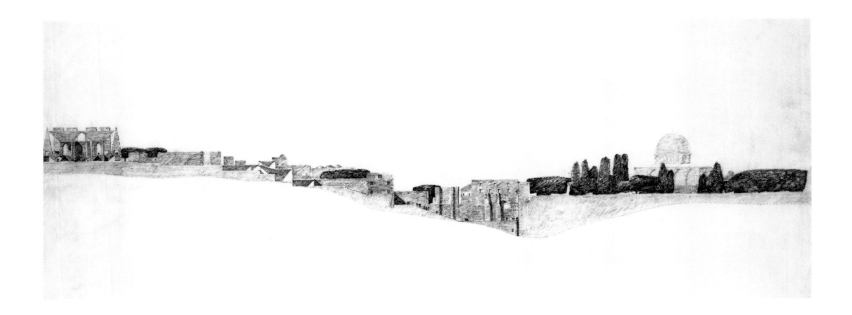

Hurva Synagogue, Jerusalem. Section through the projected synagogue, on the venerable site on the edge of Mt. Zion, and through the Central Valley, the Wailing Wall, and the Temple Mount (the Mosque of Omar is shown in outline). 1967–74

more modest one, in honor of President Franklin D. Roosevelt, envisioned for the south end of Roosevelt Island, was designed in 1973 but also never got beyond the project stage. Kahn was deeply touched by both: the first allowed him to perform his own personal act of mourning and empathy, while the second reconnected him to the New Deal era. Even a cursory examination of these projects will reveal the humility before the matter at hand with which Kahn approached his work, the constant questioning of his own as well as his clients' premises, and his sense of wonder.

That sense of wonder – at the past, at natural phenomena, at other people, at the nature of his task, even at his materials – is perhaps the secret of his greatness. It guided him to formulate his ideas in aphorisms: "a plan is a society of rooms,"[9] he would teach, and he would become famous for urging his listeners to ask the brick what it wanted to be, though he had sense of humor enough to advise students not to do so aloud on a building site.

The constant involvement with institutional buildings and the nature of public space is a refrain that runs

through his work, especially after 1945. The approach and its implications have drawn some hostile critics: "His architecture," wrote Manfredo Tafuri and Francesco dal Co in their *History of Modern Architecture*, "gives form to what in the contemporary world tends to disappear . . . : the places of worship, taste, culture. But Kahn also created architecture for institutions that are faceless, that the world submerges and annihilates. His . . . works are intent on bringing back a collective memory. In this Kahn revealed himself to be profoundly American, expressing the never-satisfied need to equip himself with secure historical points of reference. . . . But the process can only be tautological: the new bases for architecture set up by Kahn are every bit as artificial as the myths and institutions in which he put his trust."[10]

Since all architecture is artifice in the end, these last dismissive accusations seem unreal to me. In the thirty years since they were written, some of Kahn's disciples and pupils have designed some of the most important buildings all over the world, so that the approach he initiated, an approach that may well be rooted in his phantomatic reading of that zero volume of history on which he based his fertile dialogue with the past of his craft, has outlived his critics and remains a living force determining, guiding much that is best in the architecture of the present – and perhaps of the future as well.

On September 17, 1974, Louis Kahn was killed by a heart attack in the men's room at Pennsylvania Station in New York City. He was on his way back to Philadelphia from Dhaka, Bangladesh, via Heathrow Airport in London, and his papers showed only his office address. But the office was closed – it was the weekend. His body was not identified for two days.

Irony has it that at the time of his death there were more prestigious commissions in his office than ever. An Israeli government center in Jerusalem had fallen to budget cuts in 1973, but the project for the Hurva Synagogue, also in Jerusalem – the capital synagogue for Ashkenazi Jews, on the splendid hill site that overlooks the Temple Mount – was being developed, as were the Palazzo dei Congressi in Venice – a long, low building that bridged a canal and was part of the Biennale gardens – the de Menil Arts Center in Houston, and, in his home city of Philadelphia, the revamping of Independence Mall and the overall plan of the Bicentennial Exposition, which was to take place there in 1976 and in which, until the end of his life, he hoped to be involved.

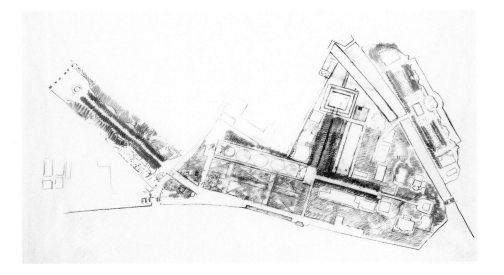

Palazzo dei Congressi,
Biennale Gardens, Venice.
Site plan with entry to the
gardens. 1968–74

Yale University Art Gallery

New Haven, Connecticut, 1951–53

Main stairway

Pages 24–25:
View from the southeast,
with Paul Rudolph's Art and
Architecture building in the
background and Swartwout's
original gallery in the fore-
ground

Kahn was asked to extend Yale University's existing gallery and museum, which had been designed by Edgerton Swartwout in 1927–28 and was the oldest college art museum in the United States. His building was also to accommodate the school of architecture and planning until it could be moved to a building that a younger architect, Paul Rudolph, was designing on a site across from it, on York Street. Kahn's envelope is rather bland – the plain brick walls are relieved by string courses that mark the floor divisions, while the glass curtain-walls are thinly mullioned in a repetitive pattern. This envelope encloses a main volume articulated into two halls, each double square in plan, separated by a narrower service area, much of it occupied by a rectangular zone for elevators, plumbing, and storage; there is also the separate regulation fire-stair. Its most conspicuous feature, however, is the concrete cylinder into which the main steel staircase is inscribed as an equilateral triangle. A link to the old building is established through a block that is a single square in plan, and is centered on the main volume. The principal entrance is tucked into the interval between the single and the double cube.

In the Yale gallery there is already a clear, almost diagrammatic distinction between the served and the servant spaces, which would become an important aspect of all Kahn's planning. It is one of his inversions of Beaux-Arts practice, which recommended that both plans and sections show blank areas into which the "construction" and the "services" could be filled. They were conventionally tinted gray or pink, while wall surfaces of the served areas were drawn in the greatest detail and rendered in brilliant color. Asserting the formal dignity of the service elements of a building while respecting the hierarchy of spaces in the plan is Kahn's deliberate challenge to the academic design method.

An early sketch shows a whole three-dimensional structure composed of tetrahedral elements, both columns and floors; as Kahn put it, these slabs "deserved" such a supporting structure, though in fact the honeycomb floors were made up of concrete tetrahedra, even if the columns and beams remained rectangular, and the string courses on the facade marked the stages in the casting of those slabs. It is perhaps the first of Kahn's works in which concrete cast in smooth plywood shuttering becomes the dominant material of the building, while the two directions of the structure allow an orthogonal as well as a diagonal arrangement of displays. The brilliant, crystalline effect of the gallery was produced by the play of light on the tetrahedra, of which the curtain wall offered a clear view – all of it now unfortunately obscured by insensitive "remodelling."

Perspective sketch from the
southeast, showing the
existing building and Kahn's
addition

Main entrance

Southwest elevation

View from the northeast

Pages 30–31:
Rear garden (north facade)

Bottom of the stairway

Stair cylinder

Views of the stairway

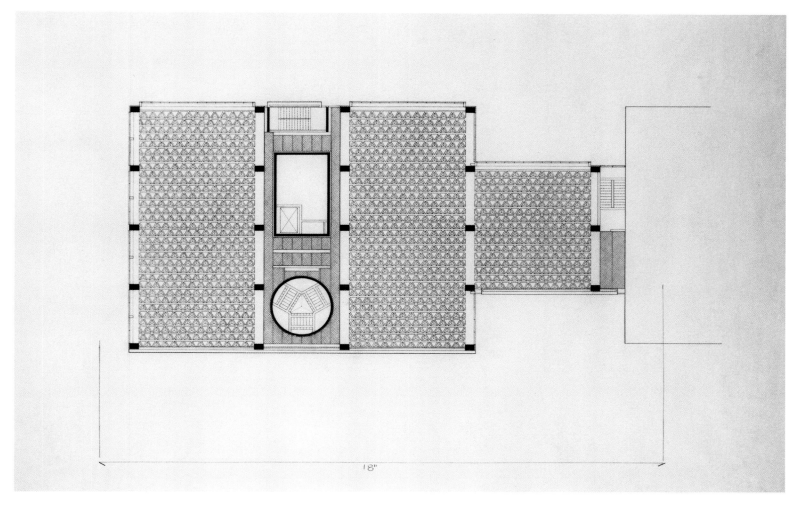

Reflected ceiling plan

Ceiling detail

Gallery space

Alfred Newton Richards Medical Research Building

University of Pennsylvania, Philadelphia, 1957–65

Main entrance

Pages 40–41:
Served and servant spaces,
clearly expressed

This is Kahn's only building on the campus on which he spent much of his life, both as a student and as a teacher. The project had a tortuous passage, patronized as it was by two departments, medicine and biology, whose demands were not always in harmony. There were several budget cuts and constant changes of program as well. The initial design went through several transformations: at one point the service towers became wider as they went up (corresponding to the increasing volume of waste air), while the structure became increasingly lighter; Kahn also experimented with arched windows. In the built design the structure of prefabricated and prestressed concrete depended on the wide cantilevers, which were obtained using standard Vierendeel trusses. They allowed free spans as well as a horizontal passage of services. The Richards is one of the rare twentieth-century buildings in which the staccato rhythm of a vertical organization dominates the whole volume.

For all that, the ordering may be considered conventional enough: an eight-story stacking of modular laboratories serviced by ducted shafts was not unusual in science buildings of the time. The overall design seems to be a systematic working of the written program, yet the sharply vertical organization of the project contrasts not only with the spread, horizontal development of the university buildings around it but also with the horizontal emphasis of most of the exemplary structures of the time, even highrises.

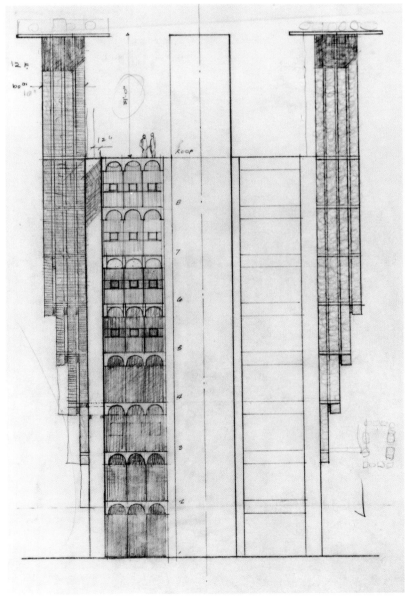

Preliminary sketch with arched
windows and service stacks
enlarging upward

Towers under construction

Moreover, the essential configuration – a group of interdependent, lightly glazed laboratory and animal-housing towers – suggested a constantly changing interior organization; this is in contrast with the taller and permanent, even monumental, ventilation and main shafts. The opposition set up the same dialectic between served and servant spaces that was diagrammatically incipient in the Yale University Art Gallery, and to which Kahn would return in most of his projects. Historical examples (the towers of San Gimignano in Tuscany, for instance) are also invoked for this building but do not seem to justify Kahn's deliberate emphasis on the formal vertical organization.

The Richards laboratories – named, after some hesitation, for a distinguished research biologist – are now the first buildings on the University of Pennsylvania campus any visiting architect or planner wishes to see. The university administration introduced a management firm at the last stage of construction despite Kahn's protests, and it would not commission another building from him. Like the Yale gallery, the laboratories have suffered from the neglect of their users, but the building received immediate appreciation from fellow architects: it was the first to be given an exhibition of its own at The Museum of Modern Art, New York, in 1963.

Aerial sketch showing the new
buildings in their setting

Entrance

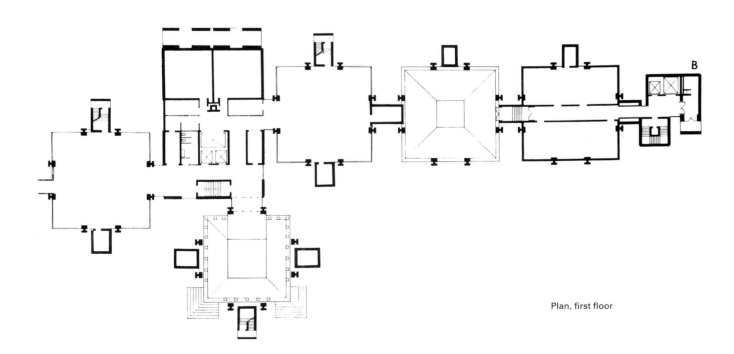

Plan, first floor

View into laboratories

Corner detail of the entrance
tower

Northwest elevation

Margaret Esherick House

Philadelphia, Pennsylvania, 1959–62

Side, with chimney

Some private houses Kahn built at about this time, such
as the timber Clever House in Cherry Hill, New Jersey,
relate to his early projects for the Jewish Community
Center in Trenton, New Jersey, and the Philadelphia
urban schemes in their structure, formal conception,
and use of the space frame as the generating form of
the building. The Esherick House, however, belongs
with the Richards laboratories. The plan is a served
near-square with an oblong attached servant area containing a kitchen and laundry below and bathrooms
above. It seems based on a 3-foot-6-inch module: the
main area is 9 by 9 (plus 1) modules, and the servant
area is produced by a diagonal on the square – a pro-
portion Kahn may have found recurring in the castle
buildings he admired in Europe. The interior volume is
articulated by a staircase, one module wide. On the
entirely glazed garden side, the exterior is dominated
by the deep reveals of the wooden window frames,
while the street elevation is much flatter – and Kahn
makes play of the narrow hinged windows against the
large areas of fixed glazing. Both sides are governed
by the play of the modules: 1, 2, 1, then by a deeper
articulation, 2 by 2 modules, and again 1, 2, 1. The
fireplace in the living room, on the narrower side of
the house, is a module wide; the window above it
opens on the tall chimney, which stands independent
of the house walls.

Front elevation

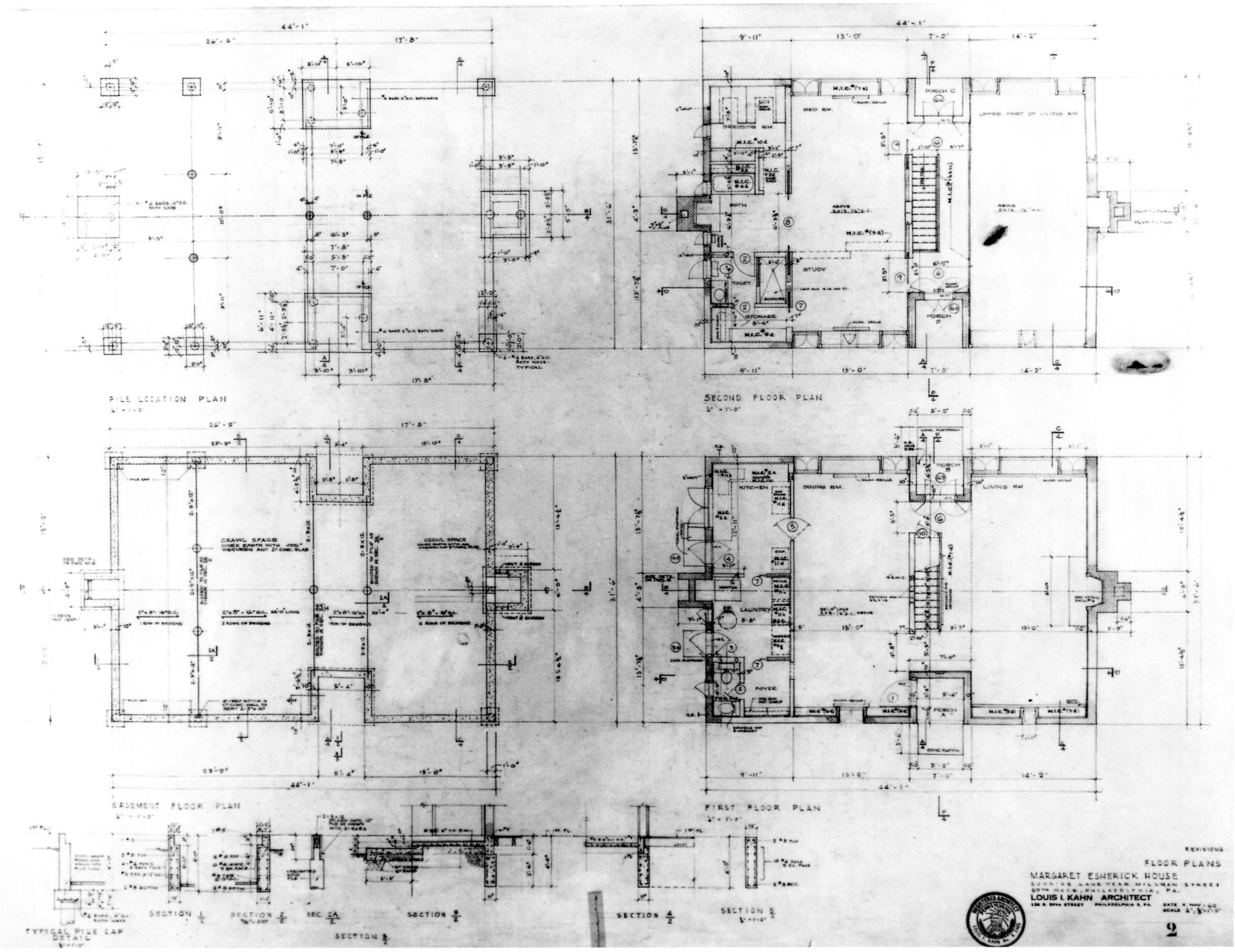

Plans

Pages 56–57:

Rear elevation with garden

Front and side

Performing Arts Center

Fort Wayne, Indiana, 1961–73

Front facade, detail

Pages 60–61:
Entrance

The theater at the Performing Arts Center commissioned in 1961 was to be part of an ambitious project to upgrade the central area of Fort Wayne, Indiana. The earliest version of the scheme shows an extensive viaduct system, which included a number of circular parking towers (adapted from the Philadelphia plan on which Kahn was working at the same time) surrounding a large-scale proposal for the town center. This system would also reconnect the city with the nearby parkland. The overall plan was then scaled down to a single group of buildings that would house a theater and a philharmonic hall, a museum, the historical society, and an art gallery, as well as a school of fine arts. By 1964 it became clear that funds would not be available, and the scheme became dormant until 1966, when work began on a reduced enterprise – the theater and the fine arts school. By 1970 there were working drawings for both, but finally only the theater was built; it was inaugurated in 1973.

In the early schemes, the isolation of the theater and concert hall from the neighboring railway lines was a dominant concern and led to the concept of an articulated double-structure building, one (the "concrete violin") inside the other (the "brick violin-case"). The notion of a building within another building – the "vio-lin inside the violin case," as Kahn put it – is one that would fascinate Kahn intermittently throughout his work. It is said to have derived from the castle ruins he admired, yet at Fort Wayne he was concerned to separate the protective, muffling function of the outer shell from the resonating effects of the molded inner concrete carapace.

Another image, that of the mask, also appears in sectional drawings of the theater stage quite early on in the project, though the startlingly facelike entry front seems to have been a late development. It is achieved by urging the brick arches and the nibbed beams that are associated with all Kahn's late work into the configuration of eyes and nose, and the main entry can therefore be read as the mouth.

Kahn's apologists and critics have found the mask analogy embarrassing, in the way abstract painters used to find the unwanted face observed in their paintings. Kahn himself seems to have said nothing about it. I find it difficult to believe, however, that anyone so acutely aware of everything visual, so conscious of the metaphoric power of a building, could have drawn that facade (as he did several times) without noting its anthropomorphic quality.

Perspective of the entire
complex. ca. 1966

Perspective of the theater

Pages 64–65:
Front and side facades

Views of stairways and adjacent areas

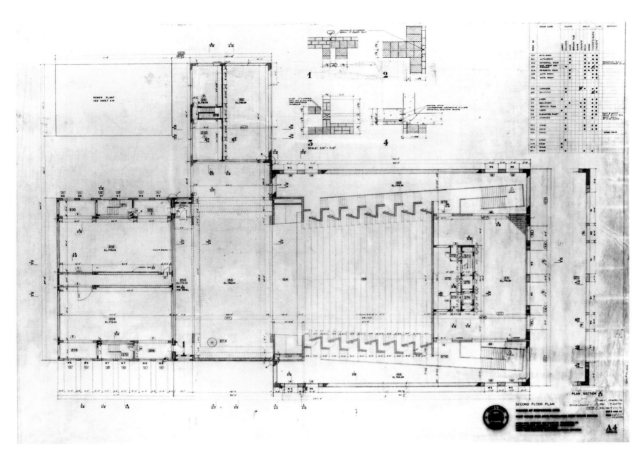

Plan, second floor

Views of the auditorium

Salk Institute for Biological Studies

La Jolla, California, 1959–65

Courtyard at twilight

Pages 72–73:
Study towers and the
courtyard, with the Pacific
Ocean in the distance

Kahn and Jonas Salk met in 1959, and there was an immediate rapport between them. Though Kahn was, in the end, disappointed in the partial execution of this project, he thought of Salk as his most perceptive client. They met because Salk heard a report of a lecture Kahn had given in Pittsburgh and proposed to consult him on how to choose an architect for his California research center; although he went to Philadelphia and was given a tour of the Richards Medical Research Building, he never got around to asking the question. Even if Salk recalls that he was not overly impressed by the Richards towers, he was clearly very taken with Kahn personally, who, for his part, was captivated by Salk's idea that biomedical research was not only an affair of professionals but "belonged to the whole population." Indeed, Salk became "his most trusted critic."[11]

The site that Salk selected for the proposed institute was just off the panoramic coastal road in La Jolla and stretched down to the bluffs overlooking the Pacific. It had been donated by the city of San Diego in 1959.

Kahn was not given a written program, but there were constant discussions between him and Salk, on the basis of which variants of the project would be elaborated. At first the proposal was for a multicenter, almost an urban, plan. Kahn envisaged two fora, or building complexes, each with its different public spaces: the laboratories on the outer edge of the site, nearest the roadway, and at the other end, on the bluff, a "meeting place" – a public square outlined by lecture theaters and a library as well as a recreation center.

In some of the early versions of the project, the road connecting the two parts would be thickly planted and have sports grounds on one side, housing on the other. The meeting place was planned as a monumental ensemble in the greatest detail, with a large auditorium as its focus, which in the final version became an amphitheater. In the buildings surrounding the main square, Kahn developed a theme that then preoccupied him. About that time he had also been asked to design the American consulate in the capital of Angola,

Aerial sketch of the entire
project, looking east

View of study towers,
laboratory block, and the
reflecting pool

Luanda, and glare was a constant problem. He considered sunscreens and *brise-soleils* to be disfigurements on many contemporary buildings. The solution he adopted was to make the enclosure a double wall, one building inside another, as it were – another device that has been traced to Kahn's fascination with ruined castles. He, however, explained it himself in terms of avoiding the glare of the sun – particularly the glare from windows inside sharply sunlit buildings.[12]

Though not as painful as it would have been in Luanda (the consulate was not built), the California sun can be sharp enough; in the project for the La Jolla institute, Kahn exploited the device by placing square buildings within circular outer shells, and circular buildings in square surrounds. This brusque juxtaposition allowed him to articulate the social center for the Salk Institute as a development of square- and cylindrical-plan solids. It was a theme to which he would return again and again.

A number of models of this part of the complex were made, but it was never built. Meanwhile, the project for the laboratories went through several stages. At one point the whole block was composed of four banks of long laboratory buildings, separated by zones of study and meeting rooms. With the Richards experience behind him, Kahn and his engineers decided to accommodate all the services in deep box-beams, trapezoidal in section, which articulated the laboratory space without dividing it. Salk found this arrangement too constricting, however, and in the final version, the area of the laboratory buildings was reduced: two multistory blocks enclosed an open courtyard, which Kahn proposed to treat as a garden. He had recently been very impressed with the work of the Mexican architect Luis Barragán, and was convinced that he was the right man to advise him. Barragán, for his part, took some luring, but when he came to La Jolla, he convinced Kahn and Salk that the courtyard should be left unplanted and act as the binding element of the two buildings,

their "facade" toward the sky, cut only by a thin water-channel, like the water-courses of certain Arab palaces.[13]

In the executed scheme the laboratories were on three floors spanned by Vierendeel trusses deep enough to provide intermediate service floors between them. They were separated from the court by a zone of small towers containing study rooms, their floors half a level above the relevant laboratory, so that stairways provided a separation and an intermediate link between them. The bulk of the building is cast-in-place concrete, the shuttering carefully jointed to make a rich surface pattern. The walls of the studies are so angled that their windows did not look into the court or at each other, but westward toward the ocean. Whereas the laboratories are faced with concrete, the study towers on the court are finished in wood siding. At the level of the courtyard, a sheltered walkway passes under the studies to turn the court itself into a cloister.

At the east, the road end of the complex, there is a grove of orange trees arranged in a quincunx plan, as Barragán had suggested, while at the west end, which faces the ocean, the central channel of the courtyard opens into a reflecting pool and – since the land drops off at this point – the water descends into a basin through a bulky gargoyle, providing a fountain focus for an open-air meeting area. The court and all the stone surfaces are paved in travertine, that honey-buff aereated stone of which so much of Rome was built, and which turns a silvery gray with time.

The institute did not have the solid financial resources on which its founder had counted. Even the laboratories, once built, could not be fully equipped and occupied for some time, and the housing and the other buildings were added later on a more modest scale and formal ambition. However, the Salk laboratories have become one of the canonic buildings of the second half of the twentieth century.

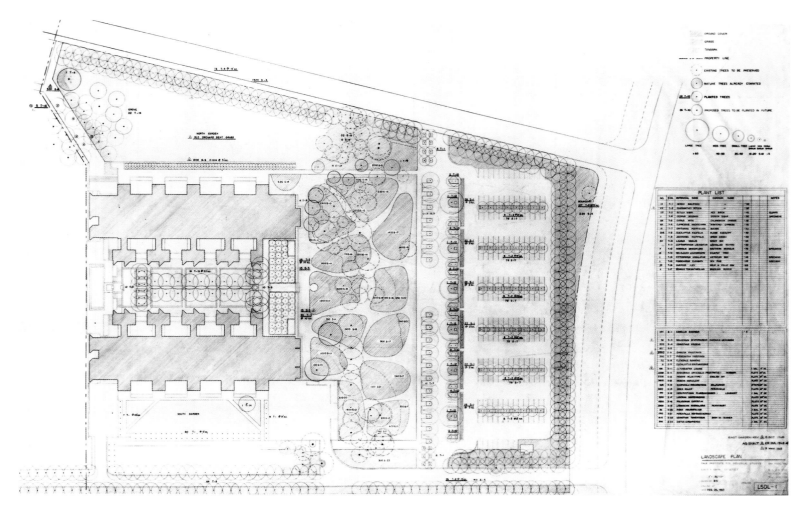

Landscape plan

Interior street of residences

View of the courtyard from a
sheltered walkway

East end of the complex

South facade of the laboratories

Pages 82–83:
View from the west of the
open-air meeting area
and fountain, with the study
towers behind

Study tower and stair

First Unitarian Church and School

Rochester, New York, 1958–61, 1965–69

Entrance; school block is at left

The Unitarian community of Rochester, New York, worshipped in a Gothic revival church that had been built in 1859 by Richard Upjohn, best known as the designer of Trinity Church in New York City. With the reputation of Upjohn in mind, and the example of that other Unitarian community who had commissioned Frank Lloyd Wright to design Unity Temple at Oak Park, west of Chicago, the Rochester Unitarians, who were threatened by development destruction, wanted a building of equal distinction to replace their church. After a search they appointed Kahn to design their house of worship and school. In 1959 a site was found. The first sketches were for an octagonal or circular building, but the one presented as a model to the congregation was for a 12-sided (almost circular, therefore) high sanctuary surrounded by a double ambulatory – signifying a varying degree of commitment to the central Unitarian tenets. The sanctuary was set at the center of a lower, square building. It had a tower at each corner in which the library, a chapel, and offices were situated, while classrooms were distributed in the remaining spaces. The building committee was uneasy with the rigid form and the unequal sizes of the rooms that resulted from this geometry; nor could Kahn himself decide on the appropriate structure for the large roof-span. He was asked to start again, but rejected the solution some of his clients advocated of two separate and linked buildings for the school and the church.

After some months Kahn designed a nearly square sanctuary/auditorium, which was also surrounded by an ambulatory. The offices and the school are grouped more loosely around it, with four lantern towers recalling the corner towers of the original project. The clerestory of the sanctuary rises above the ancillary rooms.

The main space is covered by a kind of inverted groin vault with its lowest point at the center. It is supported by an ingenious prestressed frame, within which the sanctuary is a rectangle in a concrete block, its great severity relieved by tapestries Kahn devised for it. The high lanterns cover the corner spaces left over by the cruciform vault.

The exterior of the complex is walled in brick and capped by thin concrete cornices. Kahn's fascination with the control of natural light is again evident. He invoked his design for the Luanda consulate – though Rochester, as he well knew, has different light conditions. He therefore did not have recourse to the double building, but devised a series of tall, thin windows framed by deep embrasures, which enabled him both to admit much hooded daylight and to produce an exterior as vertically articulated – in spite of its very modest height – as the Richards towers in Philadelphia without any risk of glare.

In 1965 Kahn was approached again to provide additional meeting rooms and classroom spaces. He housed them in an adjoining block into which the volume of the original porch could be extended and which continues the surface and the vertical emphasis of the first building.

Elevation sketch

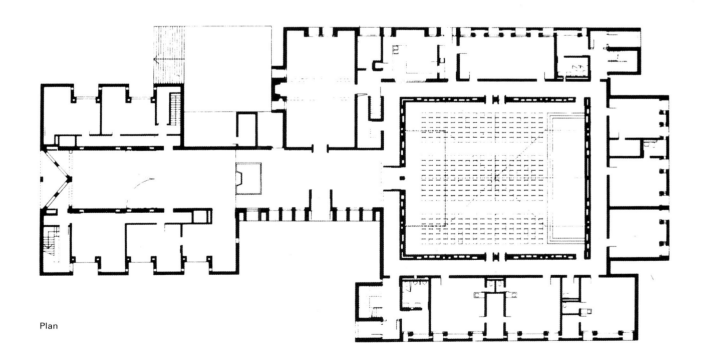

Plan

Pages 88–89:
Rear facade of the church, with
view of light towers

Pages 90–91:
Rear facade of the church

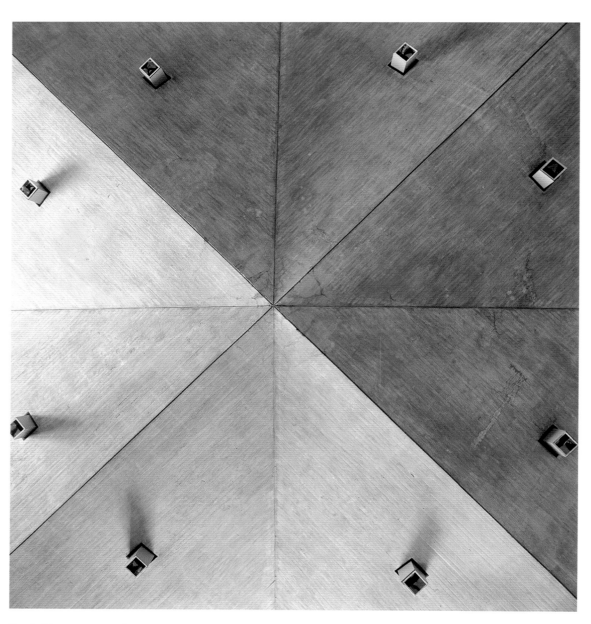

Detail of the sanctuary vault

Detail of the sanctuary
vault prestressed frame and
concrete-block wall

Doors in the sanctuary

Sanctuary/auditorium and
the organ, above

Eleanor Donnelley Erdman Hall

Bryn Mawr College, Bryn Mawr, Pennsylvania, 1960–65

Rear facade

Pages 98–99:
Dormitory units and, at right,
a clerestory lantern

The Bryn Mawr dormitory building marks another stage in Kahn's development. He was commissioned to design it by the president of Bryn Mawr, a women's college founded in the nineteenth century, even before the funds were available. This allowed some time for designing, which was slow and contradictory. Bryn Mawr custom required large public/social spaces for the use of students. In some early schemes the emphasis is on the bedroom unit, which was conceived as a grid of alternating octagons and squares, so that the resulting building has some of the indeterminacy of a honeycomb. Parallel studies for this project took the separation of social from private spaces as a starting point.

Kahn had actually been given a written program in May 1961, but finances were not secured until mid-1963. By then the main outline of the plan had been set out. There were to be three square public rooms: the main hall at the center is also the entrance space with two open symmetrical staircases, while the dining room and the living room or lounge are placed on either side. Each of the public rooms is surrounded by zones of much smaller dormitories, achieving a balance between the two divergent approaches that informed the preliminary schemes, though the served/servant relation of the other buildings is not established, even if the sleeping quarters were certainly the lowly attendants to the major social spaces.

The building is organized as three linked, square-plan parallelepipeds, each one set diagonally to the main orientation of the campus, so that they read as diamond shapes. This is a departure from much of Kahn's earlier work. The squares do not butt on each other, but overlap by the depth of the private room zone, providing the essential passage or link elements, while the corners are broken by doors and windows. The interlinking at the corners, different on each of the three floors, allows the user and visitor to sense the space as he or she walks from one public room to another almost as if it were breathing. This effect is emphasized by the top lighting, filtered by tall clerestory lanterns on the roof, not unlike those in Kahn's Rochester Unitarian church. All this allows for a new interpretation of the "building-within-a-building" type, since the inner one at Bryn Mawr is made up of the public rooms, whose volume is emphatically modeled by the concrete planes that articulate them, while the outer one is a shell provided by the "skin" of the student bedrooms.

On the exterior, the vertical articulation of the volume was maintained up to the final design by giving every bedroom a bay aligned with the campus, which made a 45-degree angle to the main dormitory building. In the definitive scheme, however, the rooms are aligned with the outer surface, and the vertical emphasis is therefore provided by clearly expressed framing walls, which are emphasized by precast concrete moldings – light gray against the dark surface of the glass and the blue slate of the panels that are the exterior facing. Brick was not allowed on the Bryn Mawr campus.

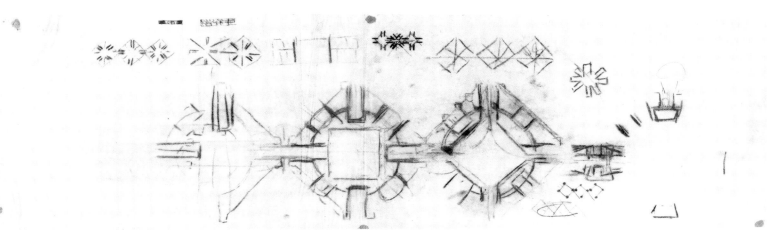

Preliminary sketches of plans

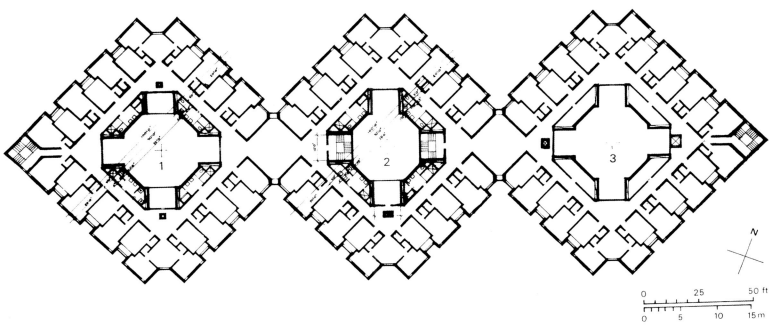

Plan

Pages 102–3:
To the left of center, the joint
between two of the blocks is
visible

Upper level of a central hall

Upper level of a central hall
and staircase, viewed from the
staircase opposite

Stairway, with a view of the
coffered ceiling

Stair detail

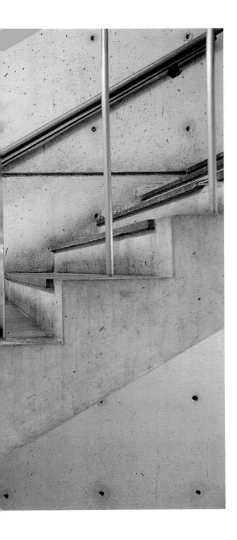

Stairway

Dr. and Mrs. Norman Fisher House

Hatboro, Pennsylvania, 1960–67

Entrance

This is one of several single-family houses Kahn was commissioned to design around 1960, most of them in Philadelphia and its environs. The Fishers had a site that sloped down to a creek, and Kahn positioned the house to overlook it. The building has a constant roof-line, but the plan is composed of two rectangles. One is a square and has the entrance hall and master bedroom at ground level and two secondary bedrooms above. The other is oblong – nearly square – a duplex room that contains the dining and living spaces and is articulated by a big stone fireplace and a kitchen alcove. In a surprise move, the two rectangles are set at 45 degrees to each other, the duplex slightly overlapping the square to create a passage between the two rectangles, much as Kahn had overlapped volumes in the Bryn Mawr dormitory building, a juxtaposition he obviously found very exciting.

The structure of the house is a wooden frame; it is faced in vertical tongue-and-groove siding. The house stands on a base of local stone, laid as squared rubble; the fireplace is made of the same stone. The garden room in the basement opens to a path descending to the creek. Kahn treated the windows of this house, as he would often from now on, either as fixed areas of glass or as openable embrasures providing an essential vertical accent. Inside the house many are finished almost as if they were pieces of furniture – a feature that would recur in Kahn's work and would allow him to create the intimate spaces that many of his contemporaries could never quite emulate.

Bridge over the creek

Entrance facade

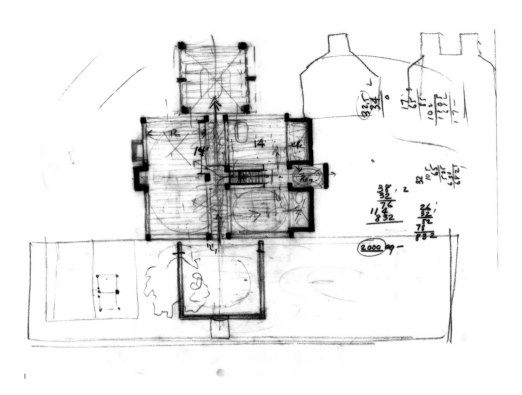

Preliminary sketch of the plan

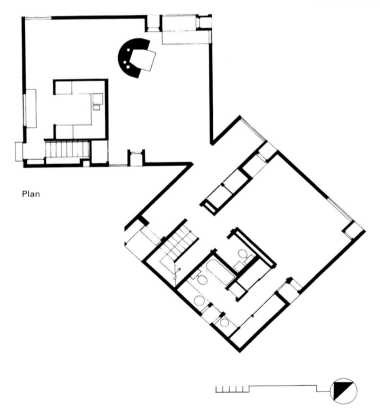

Plan

View of the house from across
the creek

Living area

Rear facade

Library, Phillips Exeter Academy

Exeter, New Hampshire, 1965–72

Central hall

Pages 118–19:
View, from the northeast, of the
library and commons

Phillips Exeter Academy is a prep school housed in a
red-brick campus dressed with prominent neo-Georgian
stone quoins and moldings. It had a university-scale
library for which a white clapboard building had acted
as a temporary home. When the decision to give it its
own permanent structure was made, the authorities
rejected the idea of a matching neo-Georgian library.
After visiting works of several leading architects, they
chose Kahn; later they added the commission for a
dining hall with its kitchen on an adjoining site. Even-
tually, both buildings would be served by the mechani-
cal plant in the basement of the dining hall.

Kahn responded to the old buildings by maintaining
the materials: brick casing, stone lintels, wood paneling.
He had always had a great love and reverence for
books, and he undertook this project – his first library
building – with great enthusiasm. The trustees and
the building committee, as well as the librarian, felt that
in Kahn they had chosen an architect who understood
their needs. They never went back on this conviction,
and for all the disputes, budgetary restrictions, and dis-
agreements, Kahn was able to achieve a work that
corresponded in large measure to his intentions, which
he stated very clearly himself:
*I made the outer depth of the building like a brick
doughnut, independent of the books. I made the inner
depth of the building like a concrete doughnut, where
the books are stored away from the light. The center
area is a result of these two contiguous doughnuts; it's
just the entrance where books are visible all around
you through the big circular openings. So you feel the
invitation of the books.*[14]

The brick enclosure is broken at each corner, so that
each face of the building can be read as a wall, though
more careful scrutiny will show it to be a row of brick
piers, increasingly slender as they rise, connected by
deep jack-arches at each floor. This modulation of the
surface enlivens and refines the otherwise rather for-
bidding cube of the building. Most of the arched opening area is taken up by a large fixed sheet of glass over
a stone lintel; this illuminates the passages and the
general reading space, and provides the diffused light
needed for the zone of stacks beyond. Inserted under
the lintel is a wooden panel broken by two small windows, which correspond on the outside to two back-to-
back carrels inside.

Although there seems to be no direct precedent for
the Exeter building, Kahn had always realized that the
lonely act of reading must be associated with the
exchange of ideas in studying. He saw it clearly incorporated in the relation of cloister to carrel in some
monastic libraries, particularly the one at Durham,
England, which he knew. Certainly Kahn conceived the
central hall at Exeter, with its huge circular openings
on four sides, as a kind of cloister, while the carrels
provide the right measure of privacy, which is emphasized by the individual window of each. The light
demarcates the three zones of the building: the brightly
lit carrels with the view, the in-between zone of stacks,
and the other suffusedly lit central hall.

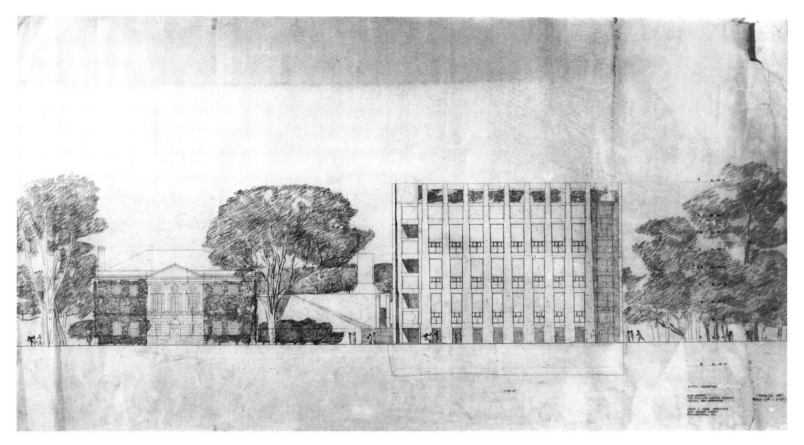

North elevation

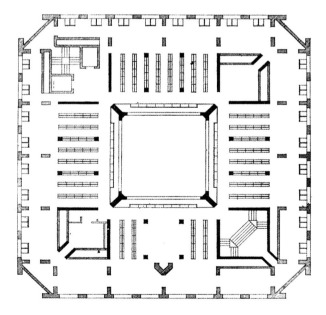

Plan, third floor

Upper level of the central
stairway

East facade

Central stairway, details

Central stair, with entrance
to the reading room below and
view into the stacks above

Central hall and ceiling

Central hall, detail

Ancillary stairway, details

Study carrels

Corner of the stacks

Olivetti-Underwood Factory

Harrisburg, Pennsylvania, 1966–69

View of the facade, showing a
faceted wall and a skylight

Pages 134–35:
Entrance, at right

When he was commissioned by them, in 1966, Kahn was the obvious choice for Olivetti, who were then the most discerning patrons of industrial building – anywhere. He was exhilarated by the demand to build a neutral space which the changes made necessary by the rapid turnover of typewriter and computer design inevitably introduced, and imagined an unencumbered industrial space. He proposed a system of columns that could incorporate a source of light, perhaps through a skylight pierced in the roof surface around the capital. Kahn and August Komendant, his consulting engineer, devised a sixty-foot-square umbrella-like unit, each one carried by a hollow column, which could, incidentally, drain the large areas of the roof surface. The corners of the roof structure are clipped so that there is a square

opening at the meeting point with the umbrellas diagonal to the grid; each one of them is covered by a lantern, which allows daylight to stream in.

The work benches (and the service ducts) could also be arranged on the diagonal, giving long, uninterrupted runs where they were required, while the more permanent and fixed planning elements – eateries, offices for management – were set to one side of the building. Since the edge umbrellas are clipped like all the other ones, the V-shaped nick that resulted allowed Kahn to articulate the perimeter wall of the building rhythmically, and to use the long, narrow windows that he favored. It makes for an unusual industrial shed, vertically striated, with a roof dominated by the pyramidions of the lanterns.

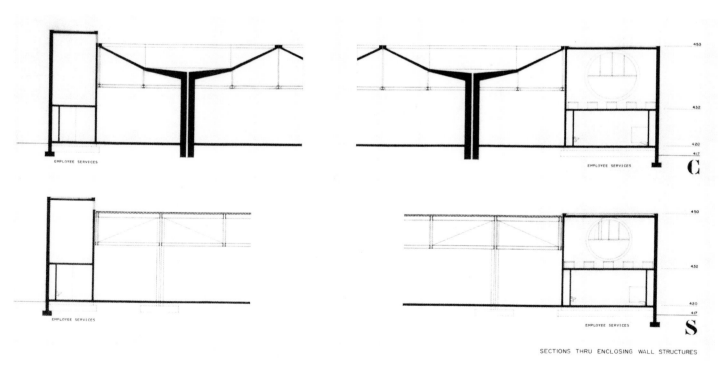

SECTIONS THRU ENCLOSING WALL STRUCTURES

Sections

Interior sketch

Views of the workspaces

Skylight details

Kimbell Art Museum

Fort Worth, Texas, 1966–72

Approach to the porch

Pages 144–45:
View of the garden, with sculptures by Isamu Noguchi

The Kimbell Art Museum was, if some of his associates are to be believed, Kahn's own favorite among his works. Kay Kimbell, an industrialist and collector (he had died in 1964), founded a trust in the city of Fort Worth to which he left his collection as well as funds both to expand it and to construct a museum to house it. He wanted it to be an outstanding building. The decision to approach Kahn was made in 1966 by Dr. Richard Fargo Brown, whom the foundation had appointed the first director of the museum. At the time Kahn was working on the Olivetti factory, the Exeter library, and the Indian projects. Building was to begin within a year, though in fact ground was not broken until mid-1969. Kahn worked on several successive plans, the first a square pierced with open courts (a long rectangle), then an "H" plan, and finally the "C" plan, the figure adopted. In all of them the consistent feature was the vaulted roofing that ran the whole width of the building. Each vault was broken at the center by a slit through its middle that allowed light to enter. Brown and Kahn agreed that daylight was to be the main source of illumination for the museum, but the powerful, glary Texan sun would have to be diffused by a baffle, so that no direct light fell on the works of art. A pierced and polished aluminum screen turned out to be the best material for it, giving exactly the sort of silver light that Kahn had wanted. It is this baffle that Kahn would later call a "daylight-fitting."

As for the form of the vault, Marshall Meyers, who was Kahn's assistant on the museum, suggested the use of a cycloid, which – when cast in prestressed concrete – could be very thin. The whole museum is covered by sixteen of these vaults, each one 22 by 154 feet, which run north-south, the whole length of the building. Between them are flat-roofed elements, which carry the services, and each vault is closed by a structural diaphragm at either end; the diaphragms are clearly separated from the nonstructural walls by a glazed slit. The concrete of the structure has been left bare, while the infill and the floors are in honey-colored travertine.

The plan divides into three units. On the south is an exhibition gallery and auditorium; on the north is space for the permanent collection (and workshops and staff facilities in the basement). Each of these two units is six vaults deep, while the central, recessed section is four vaults deep; it houses the main entry, the café and shop, as well as offices and a staff library in a mezzanine. On the park – the west – side of the building, one vault in every one of the three sections is outside the walls, as it were, and acts as a porch. The surrounding parkland is separated from these porches and their terraces by reflecting pools.

Inevitably, of course, the collection has outgrown its home over thirty years, and proposals to extend the museum by simply multiplying and repeating the cycloid vaults seem to some critics to frustrate Kahn's intention. The extension is now to be designed differently, and set in a nearby but separate location.

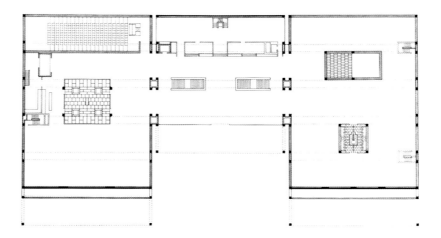

Plan

Porch with reflecting pool

Preliminary plan, oblong version

Entrance facade, at night

Main entry

Galleries

Lobby

Stair to the lobby

Stairway

Auditorium

Indian Institute of Management

Ahmedabad, India, 1962–74

Management Development Center

In 1962 Kahn was offered important work in the Indian subcontinent. The Pakistani authorities, who were involved in creating two new capitals – the western one, Islamabad, and the eastern one, Dhaka (now the capital of the separate state of Bangladesh) – invited Kahn to realize one of his most important buildings, the state capitol. He made his first visit to the subcontinent that year, and took advantage of the occasion to visit Chandigarh, the new capital that Le Corbusier had built for Indian Punjab and whose buildings he admired, though he was critical of the way the plan had been worked out.

Ahmedabad had also been a new town – in the fourteenth century, it was a Muslim foundation. During the British Raj, it became a center of the Indian textile industry, and at independence, the capital of Gujarat province. Though it is no longer the provincial capital (which was moved to Gandhinagar, for which Kahn was also asked to prepare a plan), it has, with a population of 2.5 million, remained industrially and financially vital. One of the earliest notable buildings of independent India, the Gandhi Ashram, was designed by Charles Correa and built there in 1958–63; its pyramidal roofs recall those of Kahn's Trenton bath house. Balkrishna Doshi had already come to Ahmedabad in 1954 as Le Corbusier's site architect. The latter had been commissioned to design a number of buildings in the city: the Millowners' Association, which has recently been restored; the museum, which now stands empty and derelict; and a number of private houses, two of them for the Sarabhai family.

There was by 1962 a National Institute of Design in Ahmedabad and a school of architecture connected with Gujarat University. The Indian Institute of Management, an independent neighbor of the university, was founded with Sarabhai support on the model of Harvard Business School, and Doshi, who had acted as Le Corbusier's site architect on the museum, was invited to design the entire campus. He demurred – and suggested that Kahn be invited to do it, with Doshi himself acting as the Indian link-man. It was also to be an occasion for Kahn to become the guru and teacher to the design institute, whose students could act as his assistants on the Indian Institute of Management. In fact, as work on the project began, Kahn's drawings were developed by students in Ahmedabad and sent back to him in Philadelphia. Later he would have a group of young Indian architects working for him specifically on these buildings.

As it was for the Exeter library, the monastery was again the type, the "form," as Kahn would have said, from which his design started. From the outset, a rectangular building was proposed at the center to house the library, administration, and main teaching rooms; in the earliest scheme, it seems to have been a dominant mastaba-like pyramidion, but soon it was transformed into a courtyard building. Staff and student housing was grouped on two sides of it, diagonally. Early in 1963 the project was far enough advanced for a large model to be made, but four or five further variations followed. In all of them the main *parti* was more or less maintained: a large rectangle of administration and teaching, half surrounded by student housing, with accommodation for staff and servants separated by a lake. The diagonal orientation of the houses was determined by the direction of the wind. The climate of Gujarat is tropical, the summer heat rising to 113 degrees and never falling

Preliminary project, section
through the main square

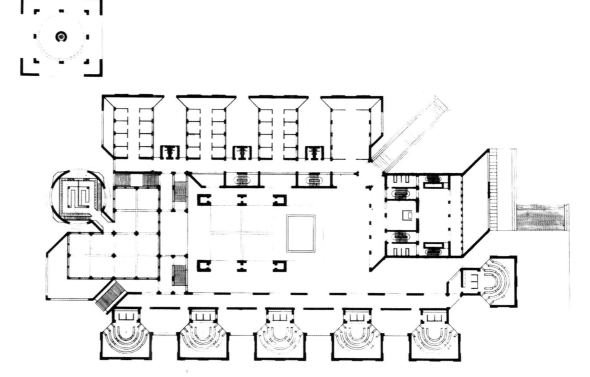

Classroom building, plan,
court level

much below 40 degrees, with violent monsoon rains in the spring. Wherever possible, therefore, the interiors were protected by deep porches and connected by covered walkways. The student hostels were equilateral, right-angled triangles in plan, the two short sides made up of student rooms, the long base enclosing a common living room; their kitchens and services were housed in a separate square-plan tower, which impinged on the triangle base, while the main stairway rises as a semicircle through the living rooms. The geometry of overlapping diagonal plan-shapes allowing for percolating passage from one kind of space to another, which seemed daring in his dormitory at Bryn Mawr, is here quite domesticated. The great circles first cut from the diaphragm wall of the Exeter library seem quite naturally at home in the brick walls of the IIM – and completely modern as well, however much they may seem to recall the great brick vaults of Roman buildings.

The principal material is handmade local brick, which was cheap, as were the concrete slabs. The vaults and arches (including inverted arches) are reinforced with prestressed concrete tie-beams. Kahn says of this kind of construction:

The brick was always talking to me, saying you're missing an opportunity. The weight of the brick makes it dance like a fairy above and groan below. But brick is stingy, concrete is tremendously generous. The brick is held by the concrete restraining members. Brick likes this much, because it becomes modern.[15]

No prestressed concrete tie-beams in Roman buildings, of course. Nor the kind of buttressing with which Kahn brings his structural walls down to the ground

at the banks of the proposed (but not realized) lake, which was to divide the student from the staff and the servant housing.

Test constructions were begun in 1964, but it took another four or five years before the main structure went up, during which Kahn simplified the design and reduced the budget. The lake, which had always been part of the design, was never dug due to fears that mosquitos would inevitably breed there. Nor was the bazaar Kahn wanted to include ever laid out. After a crisis in 1969, the collaboration with the design institute ended and one of the Indian architects who had worked with Kahn in Philadelphia, Anant Raje, took charge of the site office. He carried out essential alterations to Kahn's scheme (like the removal of the dining halls from the courtyard) and designed additional housing very much in the spirit of the project after Kahn's death. But the student and the staff housing are largely as Kahn conceived them. The water tower also remains as a landmark. Some damage to the interior has been done by the general replacement of incandescent with fluorescent light in India; this has also disfigured many of Le Corbusier's buildings.

The central building remains noble and impressive, though much reduced in area and in detail. The added accommodation and alterations have not marred the IIM. The great gestures of Kahn's design, the diagonal entrance stair, the dominant tubular volume of the library, the buttressed diagonals of the student quarters witness to the powerful imagination and formal will that made them.

Ramp between dormitories,
on the left, and the classroom
block and library, on the right

On the left, entry to the
classroom block; on the right,
the library

Pages 162–63:
Dormitories

Dormitories

Shaded street along a
dormitory block

Entrance stairway to faculty
offices and lounge, and the
library

Enclave passage

Enclave middle lounge

Pages 168–69:
The main complex: from left
to right, office block, library,
and classroom block

Classroom block and Louis
Kahn Plaza

Water tower and office block

Passage between two sets of
classrooms, opening to Louis
Kahn Plaza

Classroom-building corridor

Mr. and Mrs. Steven Korman House

Fort Washington, Pennsylvania, 1971–73

Side facade, with a view into
the living and dining areas

The Korman House, designed for a young developer and his wife, was Kahn's last built project in the Philadelphia area. Though larger than most of his other houses, it has the same rather spare and modest – even neutral – fabric Kahn favored in private houses: a timber frame structure is given an outer skin of vertical siding; only the chimneys and fireplaces are in masonry. The timber-framed windows are large and solid.

The early plans were very ambitious formally, with the kind of angled juxtaposition he had used in the Fisher House. But in the built version, they became much sim-pler. As in the other houses, Kahn maintained a clear articulation: the entry and hall separate the living from the other areas, and the "servant" rooms (in this case, bathrooms and kitchen) are clearly visible on the exterior; both the living and dining rooms are duplex. The chimneys are practically independent structures, and their detached volumes emphasize the formal integrity of the house. Kahn must be the only one of his contemporaries who managed to use such very simple, even commonplace, tectonic means and such straightforward planning to achieve the kind of ceremonious freedom that marks all his houses.

Front facade

Rear and side facades

Pages 178–79:
Rear facade

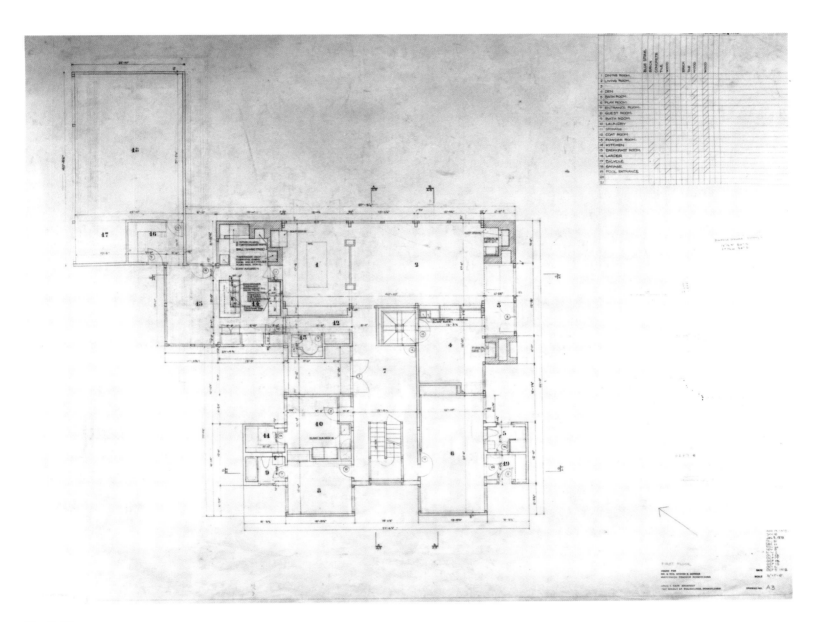

Plan, first floor

Side facade

Second-floor hall

Main stairway, view from the
second floor

Main stairway

Living room

Yale Center for British Art

Yale University, New Haven, Connecticut, 1969–74

Entrance court, skylights

Pages 186–87:
Northeast elevation

Paul Mellon, steel magnate and benefactor of (among other institutions) the National Gallery in Washington, D.C., chose to give his collection of British art and the library formed around it to Yale, his alma mater. The university decided after some debate to build a special gallery to house it, and after further deliberation commissioned Kahn in 1969. Problems arose when the university bought a site on Chapel Street, directly across from the Yale University Art Gallery, which Kahn had designed in 1951, and he envisaged the two buildings joined by a bridge. This plan brought objections from the city, which saw in it the loss of taxable commercial space (shops and lodgings) to the untaxable museum; as a compromise a number of shops facing the street were incorporated into the program.

Kahn's initial design was for a rectangle pierced by two courts. But as the plan developed, the two courts seem to have generated two separate entrances and virtually two adjoining buildings, each covered by very long, slightly curved Vierendeel trusses, with long but narrow barrel vaults spanning between them. However, even the area covered by the first scheme (and exceeded in Kahn's early and more ambitious designs) made the project too expensive, while the nature of the collection (British artists produced a great many portraits and then, from 1750 onward, an increasing number of landscapes) seemed to suggest a building designed to a smaller scale than Kahn initially had in mind.

The final, built scheme called for a single block, still pierced by two courts. One is square and rises through the four floors of the building as a light well; it is entered diagonally from the entrance terrace at ground level. The other is oblong and begins at the second floor since there is a lecture theater at ground level; within this oblong area the main stairway is enclosed in a smooth concrete cylinder, as at the Yale Art Gallery, though at the Center for British Art the stairway is square in plan, not triangular. The exterior of the building is reticulated by the smooth concrete structure, the columns growing more slender as they rise and the infill walls faced in matte stainless steel to look (or at least Kahn thought so) like pewter. Most of the light in the building is filtered through deep skylights into the courts, onto which all the galleries open. This meant that the street windows could be relatively small so that virtually no direct light need ever fall on a painting.

The structure was up and the precast beams on site when Kahn died. His wishes about the interior were well known, and he left clear instructions and drawings. Marshall Meyers (who had been Kahn's assistant at Fort Worth) and his partner, Anthony Pellecchia, finished the building, which included installing the movable, warm-colored wooden screens that give the galleries exactly the domestic feel Kahn thought appropriate to the Mellon collection.

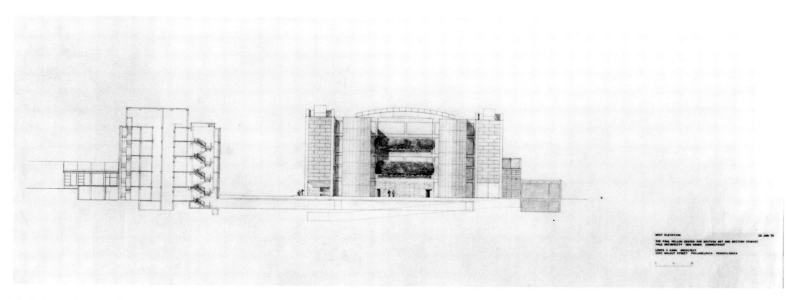

Preliminary scheme, section
and west elevation

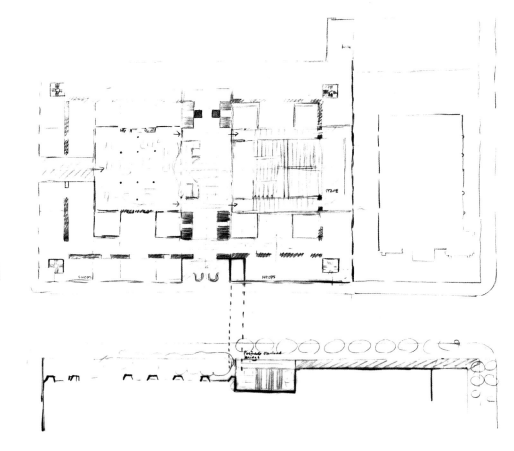

Sketch of the site plan

View from the southwest

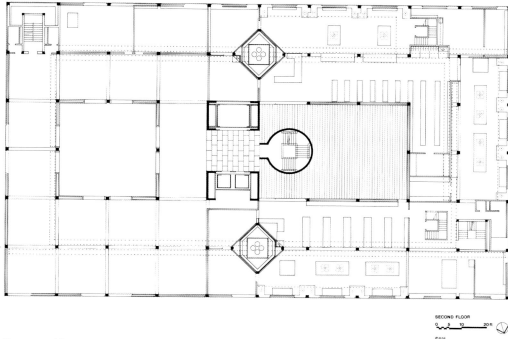

Plan, second floor

SECOND FLOOR
0 5 10   20 ft
©RM

View north, from the courtyard

Views of the entrance court

Library court

Stair cylinder in the
library court

Library court, view to the ceiling

Access from a gallery to the
stair cylinder

Stair landing

Stair and ceiling detail

Galleries

Study areas

Sher-e-Bangla Nagar

National Capital, Dhaka, Bangladesh, 1962–74

National Assembly Building,
view from the southeast

Pages 202–3:
National Assembly Building,
view from the northwest

This is Kahn's grandest and climactic project. Although it was commissioned twelve years before he died, it was to occupy him considerably during the last decade that was left of his life, and he was to meet his death on his return from a site visit there.

The commission resulted from the decision of the then-military dictator of Pakistan, Ayub Khan (who seized power in 1958) to move the center of government from its original site in Karachi, on the coast – which he considered commercial and, therefore, corrupting – inland, next to Rawalpindi, in the Peshawar foothills, and create a new capital, Islamabad, for Western Pakistan, and another for the separated eastern part of the country (the old British province of East Bengal), Dhaka. In fact, Kahn was the third choice as architect: Le Corbusier had pleaded pressure of work, Alvar Aalto was ill. Kahn was first approached toward the end of 1962, when already engaged on the Ahmedabad Indian Institute of Management project; he visited the site in early 1963.

Soon he was also asked to design the president's palace and, a little later, the state center of Islamabad. The rather awful overall plan was devised by Constantine Doxiadis, and Sir Robert Matthew (late chief architect of the London County Council) was put in charge of the architecture. A number of foreign architects were involved: Gio Ponti from Italy designed and built the administration building, Arne Jacobsen from Denmark, the parliament. Kahn was allotted the presidential estate, and when Jacobsen's project for the assembly was rejected, Kahn was asked to provide an alternative proposal. He insisted on the unity of plan and architecture, and perhaps because of that his Islamabad projects did not show him at his best, though they were immeasurably better than the vulgar and flaccid "orientalist" buildings that did go up. By the end of 1965 all his work for Islamabad had also been rejected.

The Dhaka project did, however slowly and painfully, go ahead. It had an influential advocate in Mazharul Islam, a Bangladeshi architect-turned-politician, who was determined that it should be built, and he was backed by the civil servants. For his part, Kahn saw it from the outset as a crucial project. In 1963 he had already set it as a problem to his Philadelphia students. Unlike the Islamabad plan, that for Dhaka required accommodations for the parliamentarians and their staffs as well as the appurtenances of a national assembly and a mosque for those working in the parliament buildings. They were sited on the edge of the old town, which had been made the capital of his province by Nawab Islam Khan in 1608.

The project was conditioned not only by the climate but also by the fact that the town is just upstream from the confluence of the Brahmaputra and Ganges rivers, in flood country. Planned as an equilateral triangle, it had the actual assembly building at the center of its base, with the housing for the ministers and civil servants to one side, that for the assembly members on the other. The housing is separated by lakes from the assembly building.

For some years Kahn planned the site as two "castles" that faced each other across a park: that of the assembly included the parliament and its dependencies, the supreme court, and the president's house, while that of the institutions that faced it included a sports center, a school of arts and one of sciences, as well as a market. In the end only the assembly complex was built. The site of the projected institutions complex was to be taken by the – as yet unbuilt – long, overpowering secretariat building for which Kahn had produced preliminary designs before he died. The many difficulties in carrying out a project of this magnitude were compounded by the civil war of 1971–72, which transformed East Pakistan into the new and independent state of

National Assembly Building
and connecting bridge, view
from the southeast

Bangladesh, and the site of Kahn's project then became Sher-e-Bangla Nagar: the place of the Bengali tiger.

The main design decision was to separate the assembly building from its neighbors by raising it on a platform and casting it in concrete, while the housing and the other buildings hugged the ground and were built in exposed fair-faced brick, rather like the Indian Institute of Management in Ahmedabad. Casting such a large concrete building was itself a problem – organizational as much as technical. Kahn designed its framework with this in view, but he also realized that a day's work would only produce about five feet of wall height. This was one of the reasons for setting floor-to-floor heights at ten feet, and for delineating the five-foot heights with white marble string courses; alternate ones were cast as drip molds to break the rainwater and impede the formation of moss.

The sixteen-sided main assembly chamber has eight subsidiary buildings clustered around it, four rectangular offices alternating with irregularly shaped access and "social" elements. The glazed inner buildings are sheltered from the sun by screening exterior shells, which are pierced by an abrupt, startling polyphony of circles, rectangles, and isosceles triangles of different inclination. To distinguish between the assembly chamber, which had to dominate the complex, and the prayer chamber, or mosque, Kahn set a channel of water between them and broke the axial symmetry of the buildings (which follow the cardinal points) to point the prayer hall/mosque east-southeast, toward Mecca. He also made it the most ambitiously molded element, with four "light bottles" at the corners, providing both filtered light and ventilation (not entirely successfully – it had to be air-conditioned in the end).

Roofing the main chamber presented many problems, structural as well as formal. Although building had begun in 1966, a number of designs for the assembly roof were rejected. The definitive solution – a concrete umbrella stretched between parabolic ribs – was adopted in 1971, during the independence war; it was built soon after the peace agreement. The building was not occupied until 1982 and work on the site ended in 1983, nearly a decade after Kahn's death.

Perspective sketch

National Assembly Building
and east hostels

Pages 208–9:

East hostels

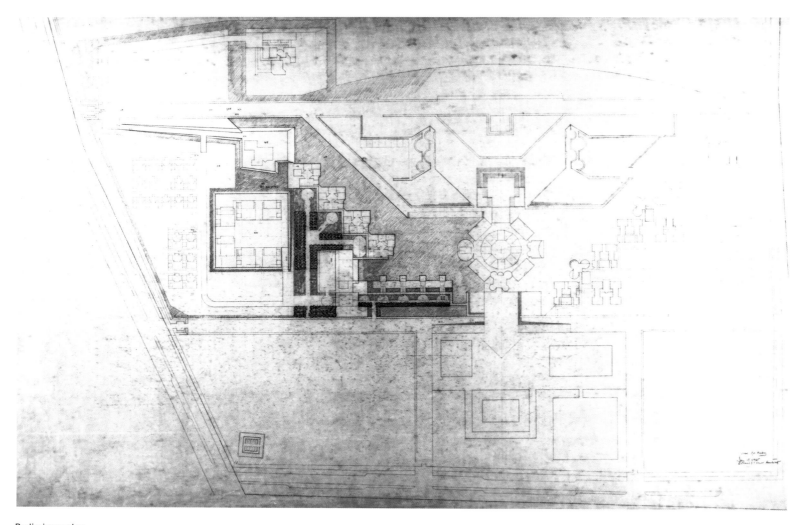

Preliminary plan

Presidential Square, National

Assembly Building

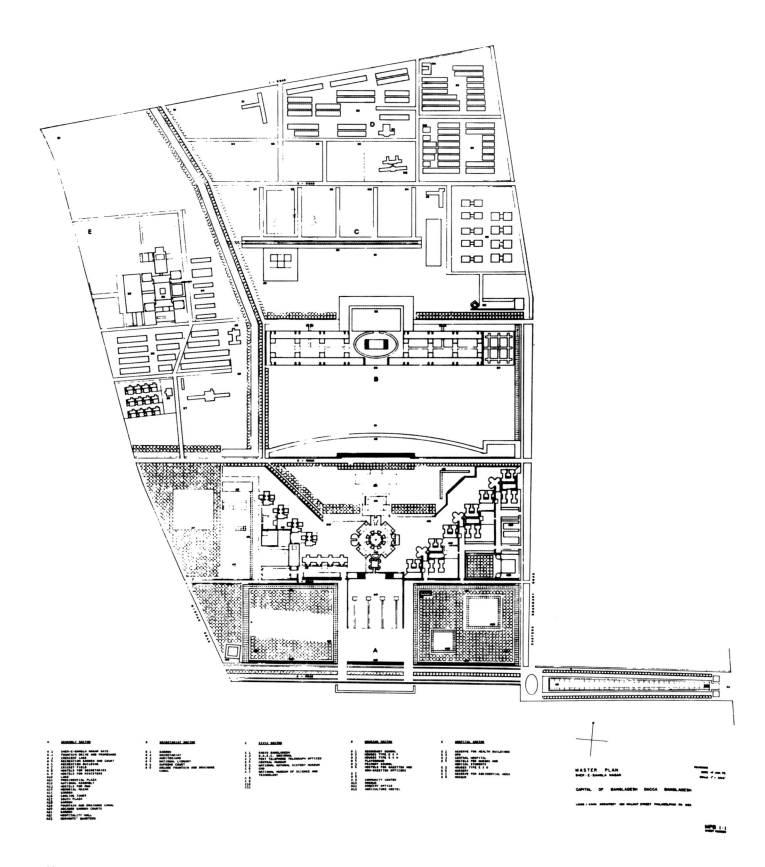

Master plan

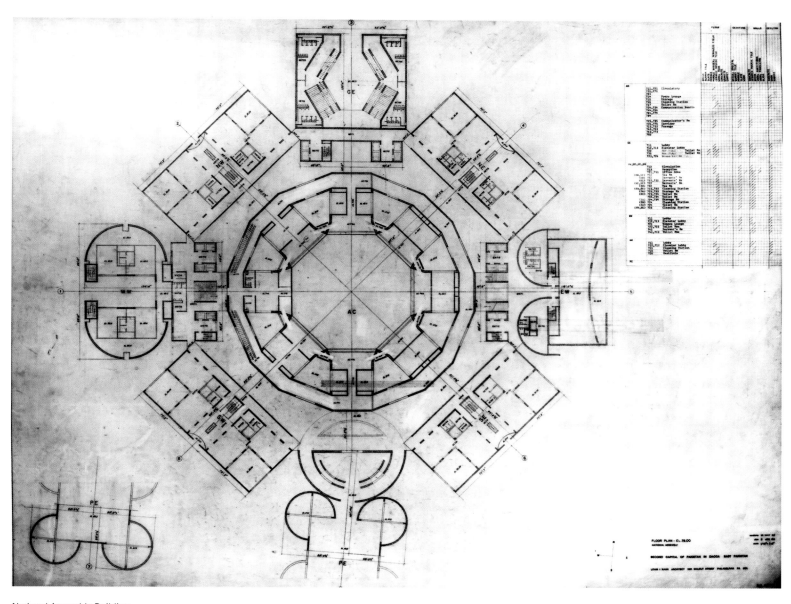

National Assembly Building,
plan

National Assembly Building,
interior and ceiling detail

National Assembly Building,
interior

Ceiling of the assembly
chamber

Notes

1   Miguel Angel Roca, *Louis I. Kahn: Arqueti-pos y Modernidad*, Buenos Aires: Ediciones Summa, 1984, pp.14ff.

2   *"L'originalité consiste à essayer de faire comme tout le monde sans y parvenir."* Attributed to Raymond Radiguet by his friend Jean Cocteau and quoted by him in *Discours de réception de M. Jean Cocteau à l'Académie Française (avec réponse de M. André Maurois)*, Paris: Gallimard, 1955, p. 18.

3   Louis I. Kahn, *Writings, Lectures, Interviews*, introduced and ed. by Alessandra Latour, New York: Rizzoli, 1991, p. 54.

4   Ibid., p. 18.

5   Interview of Dec. 3, 1972, for the *Pennsylvania Gazette,* reprinted in Latour, pp. 297ff., esp. p. 307.

6   R. Buckminster Fuller, letter to John Entenza, Apr. 5, 1965, quoted in David B. Brownlee and David G. De Long, *Louis I. Kahn: In the Realm of Architecture*, New York: Rizzoli, 1991, p. 53.

7   Peter S. Reed paraphrasing Kahn in Brownlee and De Long, p. 307.

8   Louis Kahn, talk to students at Rice University, 1964, published in Latour, p. 170.

9   Louis Kahn, quoted in *Louis I. Kahn: Complete Works, 1935–1974*, ed. Heinz Ronner and Sharad Jhaveri, 2d ed., Basel and Boston: Birkhäuser, 1987, p. 379.

10 Manfredo Tafuri and Francesco dal Co, *Modern Architecture*, New York: Abrams, 1979, p. 402.

11 Quoted in Latour, p. 206.

12 Louis Kahn, quoted in Ronner and Jhaveri, p. 127.

13 Daniel S. Friedman gives an account of the discussions in Brownlee and De Long, pp. 333ff.

14 Louis Kahn, lecture at Phillips Exeter Academy, 1972, quoted by Peter Kohane in Brownlee and De Long, p. 392.

15 Quoted in Ronner and Jhaveri, p. 222.

Acknowledgments

Although I did not know Louis Kahn
at all well myself, I am privileged
to have as colleagues and friends
many who did, and who worked
closely with him or were his students.
G. Holmes Perkins was dean of the
Graduate School of Fine Arts at
the University of Pennsylvania from
1951 until 1971, when Kahn was
teaching there. Anne Gryswold Tyng
was a most important collaborator
of Kahn's. Balkrishna Doshi, Carlos
Vallenrhat, David Polk, Miguel Angel
Roca, and Mario Botta worked in
his office at various times. Bernard
Huet and Christian and Marina
Devillers in Paris, and Julia Moore
Converse, director of the Kahn
archive at the University of Pennsylvania, have provided unstinting
support and advice. At various times
I have discussed some points with
David Brownlee and David De Long,
who organized the Kahn exhibition
that was held at the Philadelphia
Museum of Art and other institutions
in the United States and Europe in
the early 1990s.

Index

Photograph Credits

All photographs © 2001 Roberto Schezen
except the following: Louis I. Kahn
Collection, University of Pennsylvania
and Pennsylvania Historical and Museum
Commission: 16, 17, 18, 20, 21, 26, 37 top,
38, 40–41, 42, 43, 44, 45, 46, 47, 48, 49,
54, 62, 63, 68 top, 74, 77, 87, 101, 112,
121, 136, 137, 146, 147, 157, 181, 189, 191
bottom, 206, 210, 212, 213; Louis I. Kahn
Collection, University of Pennsylvania
and Pennsylvania Historical and Museum
Commission, Gift of Michael Meyers:
191 top; Anand Patel: 167

DATE DUE			
GAYLORD			PRINTED IN U.S.A.